PRAISE FOR
WHY SHE MUST LEAD

"I believe *Why She Must Lead* combines all aspects of creative ideas that women of color need to be successful today. Vasudha has created a detailed account of her personal experience and women leaders' stories that will enlighten readers with a broader perspective of the work-life experiences of women of color. I highly recommend this book to everyone regardless of their background or ethnicity so they can become the allies women of color need."

—Sage Ke'alohilani Quiamno, 2nd CEO & Co-founder of Future for Us, Award-Winning Entrepreneur, Featured in *Forbes*, National Keynote Speaker

"Our world is changing, and women of color are leading the way. *Why She Must Lead* is a much-needed investigation into how we are overcoming outdated barriers and an inspiring read for the next generation of female leaders."

—Senator Manka Dhingra, 45th Legislative District, Washington State Senate

"Astounding and powerful. That's what this book is. Women are often overlooked in various career fields and are not given the mentorship and proper guidance that can help them advance in their careers. Vasudha has touched a topic close to all of our hearts, which is equality for both genders."

—Senator Mona Das, 47th Legislative District, Washington State Senate

"*Why She Must Lead* is a true reflection of my transition into the non-profit world from a serial entrepreneur. I owned a beauty business (Meera Beauty Parlor), then moved into the garment business, followed by manufacturing cardboard boxes for exporters, and then finally managing my own advertising business. That was when I diverted my whole focus and attention to my passion for founding a non-profit and working for the community. Leadership is not just leading some people and organizations. A leader should have commitment, passion, empathy, decision-making abilities, and the skill to motivate people in a certain direction while planning daily life with due diligence. Vasudha's book will be a game-changer, an inspiring force for many upcoming women leaders to become powerful agents of change for a brighter tomorrow."

—Meera Satpathy, Founder & Chairperson of Sukarya

"Vasudha is a passionate advocate for the equal—and more—representation of women. Her dedication to equality and equity shines through in this book, and her deep commitment and long-standing work in the fight for fairness can be a lesson to many. I am excited to bring her vision of women leadership into the work I do training and readying women to run for office."

—Karen Basserman, Executive Director of Emerge Washington

"Sharma assembles interviews and reports that highlight the astonishing reality of the everyday experiences of women. A must-read for all audiences, this book empowers women leaders to manifest their goals and inspires all readers to be reverential allies for female empowerment. *Why She Must Lead* compels us to activate a vision of equity that can impact the world."

—Toshiko Hasegawa, Executive Director, Washington State Commission on Asian Pacific American Affairs

"Why She Must Lead is a must-read for any leader in the workplace and for women who want to become more impactful in their leadership. This book champions the cause of equality and connects us to build a better future together."

—Christine Gail, Best-Selling Author of *Unleash Your Rising,* Story Breakthrough Leadership Strategist, and Book Publishing Coach

"It is hard for women of color to break through social and economic barriers; Sharma's book highlights the struggles and issues women of color face daily, especially in their professional lives. Great to see this topic finally getting a bigger platform. This book comes at the perfect time when we are all trying to amplify our voices against racial, social, and gender-related biases and inequities."

—Naghmana A. Sherazi, Communications Coordinator at Gonzaga University, Office of Diversity, Equity, and Inclusion

"Vasudha is a fantastic writer and speaker. I congratulate her for successfully portraying how diverse cultures play a role in accessing opportunities for women. This book is truly about investigating the leadership gap microscopically and providing solutions. I wholeheartedly endorse *Why She Must Lead* and recommend everyone buy and read this book. My core team has all women leaders, and I genuinely believe reading it was a factor that multiplied success for us. When women start supporting each other, the sky is not the limit."

—Gunjan Kuthiala, CEO, NRI LIFE Productions and Managing Partner—Jobgini

"This book is a must-read for all women of color trying to climb the corporate ladder; we are routinely knocked down and not given the same opportunities as the average white man. We keep reaching a glass ceiling, but we are unable to break it due to structural racism. Sharma's book dives deep into the issues women of color face in the workplace."

—Heena Khatri, Racial Justice Advocate

"*Why She Must Lead* is long overdue. It gives compelling evidence for how women of color are already key players in the workplace and deserve to be recognized as such. The face of America is changing and will continue to change, and Vasudha Sharma is here to help the rest of us change with it."

—Tyler R. Tichelaar, PhD and Award-Winning Author of *Kawbawgam: The Chief, The Legend, The Man* **and** *The Gothic Wanderer*

WHY
SHE
MUST
LEAD

BRIDGING THE GAP BETWEEN
OPPORTUNITIES AND WOMEN OF COLOR

VASUDHA SHARMA

NEW YORK
LONDON • NASHVILLE • MELBOURNE • VANCOUVER

WHY SHE MUST LEAD:
Bridging the Gap Between Opportunities and Women of Color

Published in New York, New York, by Morgan James Publishing. Morgan James is a trademark of Morgan James, LLC. www.MorganJamesPublishing.com

Address all inquiries to:
Vasudha Sharma
connect@vasudhasharma.com
www.vasudhasharma.com

Morgan James BOGO™

A **FREE** ebook edition is available for you or a friend with the purchase of this print book.

_____

CLEARLY SIGN YOUR NAME ABOVE

Instructions to claim your free ebook edition:
1. Visit MorganJamesBOGO.com
2. Sign your name CLEARLY in the space above
3. Complete the form and submit a photo of this entire page
4. You or your friend can download the ebook to your preferred device

ISBN 9781631955969 paperback
ISBN 9781631955976 ebook
Library of Congress Control Number:
2021936029

Cover Design by:
Kerry Jesberger
AeroGallerie.com

Interior Design by:
Fusion Creative Works

Author Photo by:
San D. Nath Photography

Morgan James PUBLISHING Builds with... **Habitat for Humanity® Peninsula and Greater Williamsburg**

Morgan James is a proud partner of Habitat for Humanity Peninsula and Greater Williamsburg. Partners in building since 2006.

Get involved today! Visit
MorganJamesPublishing.com/giving-back

For Mom and Dad.

Your example of persistence and
simplicity forever blesses me.

For my husband, Puneet,
and my children Krish and Vansh.

You have my heart and support forever.

CONTENTS

FOREWORD

by

Dr. Aditi Govitrikar

As a medical doctor, a psychologist, a supermodel, and an actor, I have seen different sides of life. One aspect I have found common to every side is women's unnerving strength and ability to surpass limits to contribute to social progress.

I recently met one such inspiring woman, Vasudha Sharma. I came to know her as an associate producer for *Grey Stories—Desires*, an upcoming web series I will star in. We met each other through a mutual friend, Gunjan Kuithala (NRI LIFE Productions). When I heard about Vasudha's upcoming book, *Why She Must Lead*, which you now hold in your hands, I was very intrigued.

When the gender gap is mentioned today, many people are shocked to hear about it. "We see women everywhere, in every field; where's the gap?" they say. The people who belong to this school of thought, unfortunately, are unaware of mounting evidence of a continuing disparity. Although, since the dawn of this century, women have made rapid advances in the workplace and the percentage of women entering management ranks has risen steadily, progress has been uneven. Significant racial and ethnic differences have long affected the rate of women's advancement. For diverse women, entering the realm of leadership has been an imperfect revolution.

The purpose of *Why She Must Lead* is to amplify women's voices, especially those from diverse backgrounds who have fewer opportunities than men. They have to break through what feels like a concrete ceiling to succeed. I believe Vasudha has all of the right qualifications to write this book because she has faced numerous setbacks after coming to the United States from India. She is a great leader who has been informed by her own experiences as a woman of color, as a first-generation immigrant, and as a mother. Her goal is to share her story and her interviews with other women to raise awareness of gender gap issues and motivate women to continue their fight against disparities. It is time her voice is heard on a larger platform, so people, like you and me, can pave the path for other women to rise and shine.

This book will help you understand, through the eyes of women with diverse backgrounds, why women are mostly missing in the corner office. Vasudha argues that women do not voluntarily choose to miss out on opportunities to lead. Instead, flaws in the system keep filtering out women who desire to rise. Unless we pay attention to the experiences of diverse women in the workplace, these flaws will only increase the leadership gap.

Women of color have come a long way, and now is the time for them to be represented fairly in key positions. *Why She Must Lead* talks about all the problems we women of color face in the work environment. It also talks about how we can solve this problem together by finding and creating allies among both males and females, raising awareness of the need for mentorship and sponsorship, and defining workplace goals to make inclusion imminent. I, like many others, did not achieve success overnight. I faced similar barriers, including the maternal wall, the pay gap, and so on. But the lessons I learned have inspired women across generations. That is the beauty of a woman who is ready to lead; she charts her path based on the journeys other women have endured reaching the sky.

This book initiates a dialogue among us about how we can understand modern-day feminism and use an evidence-based approach when forming an opinion about the topic of "Why she must lead."

It compels readers to take action through simple behaviors that can influence and contribute to equal opportunities for all.

INTRODUCTION

Ever since I entered the workforce as a professional more than twenty years ago, I have felt obligated to write this book. But interviewing women from different levels and fields and capturing their perspectives was a daunting task, so I did what any committed author would do. I took my time, reaching out to every avenue I could before I started writing.

Two main nudges convinced me to write this book. The first occurred when I was a student and trying to find a female role model; I was always intrigued and baffled by the mystery of why the world has so few women leaders. Unfortunately, that situation is still true decades later. *Why She Must Lead* is an effort to uncover the deepest layers of the global issue of gender inequity in leadership. In the late twentieth century, women rapidly entered the workforce. The gender wage gap narrowed, sex segregation in most professions considerably declined, and the percentage of women climbing the management ranks steadily rose. Progress has been uneven, however. Significant racial and ethnic differences, along with the fundamental issue of gender, have long impeded the rate of women's advancement. When researching this disparity, I found the data frightening. At this time, more dialogue and more research are needed to understand fully the different barriers to leadership that exist for women from diverse backgrounds. I hope this book helps to build momentum toward that goal.

My second nudge to write this book came from personal insight. When I immigrated to the United States fifteen years ago, I dreamt of shattering the glass ceiling in the world's most powerful nation. In 2007, I began my first job as a full-time therapist. A few months later, I read that *Forbes* had named Indra Nooyi, the Indian American female CEO of PepsiCo, the world's third most powerful woman. That achievement made me feel my dream to see women in top positions was finally coming true. But when Nooyi exited as PepsiCo's CEO in October 2018, it left us with just one other woman of color as a CEO in the Fortune 500. It was alarming to know that in recent decades, women's overall gains in leadership had slowed.

To make my dream of seeing women of color fairly represented in leadership around the world come true, I dug down deep into my personal experiences. I was convinced we needed to bring the experiences of underrepresented women into the light to diagnose the reason for their absence in decision-making positions. More importantly, I wanted to highlight the need for understanding the critical issues for women of color throughout their career trajectory, from hiring to their advancement and from job satisfaction to retention. Don't get me wrong. I am not advocating for C-suite jobs based on mere identity. I genuinely believe in a fair merit-based system for appointments. But unfortunately, that's not all it takes for women of color to advance. They must face not a glass, but a concrete ceiling with multiple layers of challenges before they can reach the top.

In this book, I have attempted to highlight the uneven path to leadership for women of color. I have addressed the enormous gap between leadership opportunities and women from diverse backgrounds. If we compare the United States to the rest of the world, we see that the difference is widening between American women and their counterparts in peer nations. The United States is ranked thirty-fourth in women's education on the World Economic Forum's 2020 Global Gender Gap Index[1] of 153 countries; it ranked twenty-sixth in women's economic participation and opportunity and eighty-sixth in women's political empowerment. Bringing attention to these numbers is essential. Through interviews, discussions, and observations, I have put together clues and ideas to help us reach gender parity and highlighted areas for companies to focus on to help broaden the talent pipeline and make it more inclusive.

In Chapter 1, I will talk about how I found feminism inside me and my journey to find my purpose. My goal is to make the reader part of the vision by showing them the bigger picture: Equity is a human right. In Chapter 2, I will share barriers and biases we need to identify and overcome by cultivating behaviors that sow the seeds of change. Chapter 3 is about identifying the contrast between recent gains in the number of women in senior leadership and how women continue to be underrepresented at every level, which can cause a shallow talent pool and fewer opportunities for women to benefit from advancement. Chapter 4 is about steps to promote fairness and inclusion and why it is vital to attain equity. Chapter 5 speaks about how a step-by-step push is needed not just at the recruiting level but also with retention to ensure every woman in the job market has the right support to achieve her potential. Chapter 6 speaks about the current lack of mentorship and sponsorship for women of color and why it is crucial for leadership. Chapter 7 is about the buzz and

1. World Economic Forum. "Global Gender Gap 2020." Retrieved from: https://www.weforum.org/reports/gender-gap-2020-report-100-years-pay-equality/.

myths around the word "empowerment" and why the message can be misleading. Chapter 8 is about discovering male allies and how to grow male advocacy for women in the workplace. Finally, Chapter 9 encourages every successful woman to pay it forward and unite in supporting leadership among people at all levels.

Every chapter has a self-reflection exercise at the end to allow readers to pause and reflect on their own experiences and observations. The goal is to enhance our ability to understand ourselves, to develop insight and motivations to take action for equity. The exercises are also meant to help readers explore their values in moments of doubt and uncertainty.

This book is also meant to inspire women to lead. It encourages women in leadership positions to realize that everything they do affects the people around them and their families and communities. I hope that this book will create a two-way ripple effect between those who have influenced us and those we influence as leaders, thus creating greater influence and positive change within and far beyond ourselves.

Vasudha Sharma

CHAPTER 1

FINDING YOUR WHY

"A woman with a voice is, by definition, a strong woman. But the search to find that voice can be remarkably difficult."

— Melinda Gates

If you read the word *journey* from a literal perspective, it ends with a "Y." However, the journey of this book *begins* with a "*why*." You must be wondering why I am saying so. I believe this book is a quest to dig into the characteristics of female leadership and to understand the necessity to promote it. Whenever I think about female leadership and women's empowerment, a question comes to mind: *Why are there so few women leaders in the world?*

I ask this question because I want you to ponder this *why*. The journey of this book is not only mine but equally yours. I want to walk side by side with you on this journey. I think the primary reason there are so few women leaders is because of thousands of years of male dominance. It is based mostly on brute strength and the male's need to keep the power and privilege he has enjoyed for millennia by creating an almost global glass ceiling. One of the greatest disparities in the world is the gap between abilities and opportunities.

This leadership gap is a challenge women face even in the world's most developed nations. My origins influence my perspective on this issue. Let me begin with a story from decades ago when I was a little girl living in New Delhi, India, with my parents.

In the early 1980s, Indian was in its adolescence as an independent nation. India declared its independence from British rule in 1947. During the independence movement, women freedom fighters contributed a great deal to the fight for the rights of the Indian people. Female freedom fighters' contributions were widely acknowledged. The first Indian Constitution, formulated in 1950,[2] gave equal rights to women based on the female freedom fighters' efforts. The constitution considered women legal citizens and equal to men with the same rights to freedom and opportunity. This perspective, however, was more in vision than in action. Indian society has historically been predominantly patriarchal. Indian women, who fought equally in the struggle for the nation's freedom, suffered the most in independent India.

The year I enrolled in kindergarten, it was uncommon for most females in India to receive a quality education or career growth. Fortunately, I was raised by very progressive parents. My nuclear family consisted of my dad, a schoolteacher, and my mom, a bank clerk. In the 1980s, Delhi was still a city with a substantial working-class, interspersed among the business class population, with a sprinkle of affluent residents on the south side. Almost 50 percent of the population resided in slums and unauthorized colonies without any civic amenities.[3] I was too young then to understand the facts

2. National Portal of India. (2020). Constitution of India. Retrieved from: https://www.india.gov.in/my-government/constitution-india.

3. R. Max & R. H. (2019). Urbanization. Our World in Data. Retrieved from: https://ourworldindata.org/urbanization#share-of-people-living-in-slums.

and figures. However, when I grew up, I did some research. I was surprised to know that in India in the 1980s, the Gross Enrollment Ratio (GER)—a statistical measure used in education to determine the number of students enrolled in school at several different grade levels (like elementary, middle school, and high school) and the ratio of eligible students to those attending school—was for girls between 88 and 93 percent at the primary level.[4]

For the secondary level, the ratio fell considerably to only 45 percent female participation.[5] That was a considerable decline. And the exciting thing is, it only increased by 1 percent during the entire decade. The following bar graph clearly illustrates the difference.

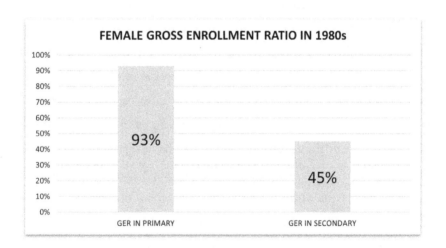

Even in India's capital city of New Delhi, women faced many social and cultural obstacles when it came to organized education. The Child Marriage Restraint Act was passed way before I was born in 1929 and raised the minimum age at which a female could be

4. The World Bank. (2020). School Enrollment Primary Female. Retrieved from: https://data. worldbank.org/indicator/SE.PRM.ENRR.FE.

5. The World Bank. (2020). School Enrollment Secondary Female. Retrieved from: https:// data.worldbank.org/indicator/SE.SEC.ENRR.FE.

married. According to this act, the minimum age for females was increased to eighteen.[6] However, decades later, in the 1980s, early teen marriage was still quite prevalent, particularly in North India.

I sometimes wonder about the usefulness of such acts. When the general population is not ready to implement them, is it worth passing the laws in the first place? It is said that the only consistent thing is change, but people rarely agree to change or voluntarily step out of their comfort zones. They do not realize how harmful their resistance to change is for the people around them.

During my growing years (the 1980s), I witnessed many women treated as if they had no control over anything related to them. They had no choice or input when it came to marriage, career, or life. Women had no voice at all. Women themselves had no value. The dowry was the criteria on which to judge their worth. The higher the endowment, the better marriage proposal they could get. In male-dominated societies, which make up most countries, I am sad to say, women face inequalities even today in every aspect of life—education, healthcare, resource distribution—everything.

This creates a paradoxical society, where, according to the law, women were equal, but by the norm, they are sacrificing their ambitions and careers. This situation was very evident during my school years. The school was more than ten miles from my home, so my family decided to put me on a private bus service. The bus got me there early and picked me up late. I spent before and after school time inside the school compound. There, I would see many parents, especially mothers, drop off their kids. Some mothers even stopped by in the middle of the day to deliver fresh, hot lunch to their kids. After school, I would see many of my friends run to their moms

---

6. The Child Marriage Restraint Act, 1929. Retrieved from: http://wcdhry.gov.in/download/laws-for-children/.

to be escorted home. As I boarded my bus to go back, I saw many mothers waiting at bus stops to pick up their kids. These affectionate sights made me feel upset and insecure. I also wanted my mother to treat me the way other mothers treated their kids.

I asked my family why I was denied this privilege. My parents gave me two reasons: 1) My mom had a full-time job that prevented her from being there when I returned home, and 2) My dad was already there since he was a teacher in a different school, but he got home at the same time I did. I always wondered why my mom could not be a teacher and my dad, a bank employee. No, do not get me wrong. My dad was indeed a great and very attentive father. However, I was quite young at that time and could not understand the nature of their shared responsibility of working parents to run a household. I believe it was hugely due to what I saw outside in general. Working women with full-time jobs were few. Their support system, therefore, was even sparser. Even in my household, my mother always discouraged the idea of me having a full-time job. She wanted me to look for career options with greater flexibility.

"You must try to become a teacher," she often said.

"You must try to become a doctor," my father would say.

In their disparity, I could not decide what I wanted to be.

"If you are a teacher, you can come home in time to take care of your family without the need for backup care. If you are a doctor, you can run a clinic with flexible hours and balance your family life," my parents would reason with me sometimes.

"IF THE FUTURE IS A ROCKET SHIP,
THEN DREAMS MUST BE THE LAUNCHPAD
TO REACH THE SKY."

In my present life, I often say, "If the future is a rocket ship, then dreams must be the launchpad to reach the sky." Of course, you need the fuel of hard work and training, but your aspirations must launch you. Unfortunately, the idea of following my heart and dreams was nonexistent when I was growing up. Frankly speaking, most households preferred practicality over following dreams. Working-class parents pressured their children to study science. They believed choosing science electives increased their children's chances of having stable careers. That is one reason why we see lots of engineers and doctors from India immigrate to the rest of the world.

My formative years were full of growing pains, not just physically, but mentally. It was because I was a dreamer. I understood practicality, but I wanted more. I had seen my mom struggle with balancing family time and work, so I realized her logic about career options. However, I still felt something was missing, not just at home but in the choices available to me.

After high school, as suggested by my parents, I worked toward becoming a physical therapist. I accepted the path my parents chose for me because I had some passion for healthcare. I enjoyed the course and made lifelong memories during my college dorm life, which was all girls. Oddly, I found the ratio of girls to boys was 5 to 1. In contrast, the pharmacy school had the ratio flipped with more males than females. I always wondered whether my mother had been right, and females were opting for physical therapy because of the possibility of having a clinic with flexible hours versus working a company job. It was an intriguing thought.

After completing my last term, I moved back to Delhi to do my internship. Arranged marriage was still a widespread practice, and my dad was worried about finding the right match for me at the so-called "right" time. It all boiled down to practicality. It was widely accepted that one's early twenties was the "right age to marry," and I was already running behind. Frankly speaking, I enjoyed the process of meeting prospective life partners, but I lacked the self-awareness to ask myself, "Am I ready?" And the even bigger question was, "Do I even want to?"

Regardless, amid all the hustle and bustle of family-arranged dates, I finally met Puneet. His family had been friends with mine for generations, but I had not seen him before. He was visiting India on vacation from his job in Los Angeles. Just like many Indian immigrants, Puneet worked at an information technology company as an engineer. I liked him at our first meeting, although we hardly spoke to each other because a dozen family members surrounded us. I wanted to talk to him in private, but I was not sure how to make that happen.

A few days later, Puneet invited me for an ice cream at a nearby market. I was surprised by his call. I had no idea what he thought about me. Nonetheless, I went to meet Puneet, and the casual meeting turned into a wedding proposal. I know how it sounds. But that is how it was back then and maybe still is in our culture. There was not much "dating" involved in arranged marriages. Good careers and great backgrounds outweighed compatibility or preferences. The social norm was to "settle down" at the "right time." There was no time for dreaming, thinking about what might be, or questioning why things were how they were.

When I got married, I felt like I had entered a time machine and landed in the future—where I had no idea where I was and what I was doing. I moved to L.A. from New Delhi. Puneet had no vacation time left for a honeymoon since he had to take three weeks off for our wedding in India. Left alone in an apartment for most of the day, I had no clue where to begin.

In 2004, I was in the country as a dependent accompanying my working spouse and could not apply for work. I was dependent as I had no Social Security number, no credit cards, and no car to drive. Worse, I spoke English with such a heavy accent that I did not want to leave the apartment to talk to anyone. Puneet advised me to apply for my physical therapy credentials, so I could get a license to practice in California; then, maybe an interested employer would sponsor a visa. Hopeful I could start my career, I did what Puneet suggested.

However, my job search results were beyond shocking. The difference in education systems between the two continents was as distinct as night and day. US-based evaluators deemed my Indian college transcripts insufficient. According to the report, I was fifty-four credits short, including missing credits in fundamental physics and chemistry with a lab. They did not even consider me a high school graduate, although back home, I had been awarded my bachelor's and had been working in a reputed hospital's rehab department. It was a very disappointing situation. The United States needed physical therapists, yet I could not even apply for a job in my field.

Sadness started to take a toll on me. However, the emotions associated with enlightenment were even more robust. I knew what I wanted and why. And so, I began that struggle.

I had already lost a year trying to transfer my credentials to the US market, so I decided not to waste any more time and quickly applied to El Camino Community College, signing up for classes in physics and chemistry. The school was about forty-five minutes away from where I lived, and I had no car. Taking the bus was a two-hour commute one way. I felt like I was back in primary school, traveling on the same buses daily, coming home alone, with assignment deadlines, labs, quizzes, and whatnot. The only difference was this time, I was busy studying everything but physical therapy (PT) so I could re-earn my credentials and practice as a therapist—something I had already earned in India. Sound confusing? It was for me, and the fight for clarity was on.

It took another year and an array of tests and courses to fulfill the credit requirements and have my education recognized as substantially equivalent by a credentialing agency. This equivalency, in itself, was a tough milestone to reach, but it would be worthless if I didn't pass the exam. Taking the national physical therapy exam (NPTE) was an important step toward receiving my physical therapist license in the United States.

The first-time pass rate for graduates of non-US PT programs was not very encouraging. It was below 20 percent. To make matters worse, I realized every state had its eligibility criteria, and the NPTE score was only one part of it. This fact was significant because without a Social Security number on an H4 visa, even if I passed the NPTE, I would still not be eligible to apply for a license in California. This awareness meant that, if everything went as planned, I would have to move to another state to get a job. Since Puneet and I had been together for only two years, deciding to live apart from him that early in marriage would not be easy.

One evening after dinner, Puneet said it would be best to take the NPTE through the state of Idaho because, with a dependent visa, I could not apply in California. I was shocked to hear about the discrepancy in the application process.

"So, should I apply only to take the test, or do you want to move to Idaho?" I asked him. "But, you told me that you couldn't change jobs because of your green card application status?"

"I can't move, but you must," he replied. Something broke inside me when he said that. He went on to say, "You wouldn't just want to hold a license and hang it on a wall, would you? Of course not."

"But I don't want to move away from you just for a job," I said.

"I know, but you have to make a choice, honey," he replied. "We can still find ways to be together, but the choice is yours."

"Okay. Let me think about it," I said.

When I first considered moving ahead in my career by becoming a traveling spouse, I had cold feet. My cultural observations had taught me that women must follow men wherever the man chooses to work. Women must find work wherever the man takes them. Today, I still think it is excellent if couples can work that way. However, it should be a choice, not just something women are supposed to do. At the time, I was going by the norms and examples of the society I had lived in. I believed in women sacrificing their careers for their families without question. I knew little about feminism or if it even applied to me.

A few months after this conversation, I passed the NPTE in my first attempt and landed a job in Lewiston, Idaho, as a traveling therapist while my husband was still in Los Angeles. I do not regret my decision to follow my heart for myself at all. I would later make similar decisions thanks to Puneet and that conversation, which opened me up to the concept of choice and breaking norms.

Thirteen years later, I am a proud feminist. Puneet introduced me to feminism. My husband made me understand that being a feminist is about equality. In no sense does it mean women are better than men or deserve more than men. It means every woman has an equal right to speak, have a vision, have a voice, and be able to use it to make choices about how she lives her life. Men and women must work together to fight the biases that have created inequality and barred women from achieving their potential.

MY HUSBAND MADE ME UNDERSTAND THAT BEING A FEMINIST IS ABOUT EQUALITY.

This insight solidified into conviction when I started meeting women struggling here in the United States and began to understand the inequity they faced. But that is not who I was thirteen years ago when I said, "I don't want to move just for a job." Then I was full of gender bias. However, my conversation with Puneet played a considerable role in my becoming intrigued by gender issues. It triggered guilt, but fighting that guilt opened avenues to success. I believe guilt can be good or bad. Good guilt helps you be accountable for your behavior. It helps you when you need to apologize. It also helps when you need to accept an apology from others and grow forgiveness in your heart. Bad guilt, on the other hand, is more devastating than the act itself. It comes from ignorance and lack of vision. It throws you into self-pity and, eventually, leads to low self-esteem. Women sometimes get in the habit of self-blame when a problematic situation arises. They want to jump on bad guilt and blame themselves. I was no exception to this feeling at the start of my career in the United States. Only by changing the focus on my *why* could I get rid of the bad guilt.

Finding my *why* made me realize that the barriers I perceived around me were products of biases and unreasonable desires to blend in. The reason I worked hard to get my license was so I could apply my knowledge and skills to serve patients. It should not have been mixed with landing a convenient job or getting the license as a medal to prove my worth to my family. I wanted to be an example for future immigrant therapists who run into similar barriers when they start a new life after marriage.

Most people try to overcome personal barriers by looking up to their role models. And often, the search for a role model begins at home. Mothers usually play an essential role in empowering their daughters. My mother would often talk to me about social justice and push me hard academically, but she could not completely erase gender biases from our family. For example, she always discouraged the idea of a woman having a full-time job and raising a family at the same time. I wondered at the irony of her doing exactly that. Nevertheless, she did not project unhappiness. I asked her questions like, "Are you going to take early retirement like some of your friends?"

She said she was not sure. I was around ten years old at that time, and my brother was five. Her logic was that it was hard to make ends meet in a big city without a steady income from both partners, so quitting was not a good option, but compromising career advancement was. "I will try not to take a promotion or higher responsibility. That way, I can strike a balance. I can sacrifice a corner office for my family." It was her opinion.

At that age, I understood her desire to find time for us, but I could not grasp her dilemma over the obstacles she faced. It was interesting for me to learn about her. Being a human, my mother was not perfect. She had many flaws, but she did not let her flaws overshadow her strengths, and I think that's important. As a kid, my mother was my first example. She very much influenced me. I learned from her that hardships and obstacles are inescapable. We will have to face challenges. We even have to fail on our journey to success because that is how the world operates. However, trials and tribulations build strong character. They must not stop us from trying to achieve or become successful if that is what we want—like my mother wanted to keep doing her job after becoming a parent. She had plans and dreams regarding her career and family, but all her plans did not work out due to the poor work-life balance of working mothers of those times.

> MY MOTHER SHOWED ME HOW SUFFERING
> AND OVERCOMING EXIST TOGETHER.

Nevertheless, she never lost hope. She knew how to join the pieces and solve problems. My mother showed me how suffering and overcoming exist together. I think I got my *imperviousness* from her. Challenges and setbacks are part and parcel of life. However, our resilience and ability to accept failure and turn it into an opportunity is what makes us stand out. My mother's example made me believe I was destined to achieve what I found worthy of achieving. Her life inspired me to find my *why*.

SEARCHING A SHALLOW POOL

Here is where leadership comes into the picture. Female role models are vital to breaking gender biases for every person in the world. My mother did not have similar role models. She mentioned that a lot of women in her time were inspired by one famous Indian woman, "Rani Laxmi Bai." Rani's confidence in discovering her *why* and her ability to lead an army of men against the British to free her people is an extraordinary example of a strong-willed woman's potential to beat the odds.

Rani is famously known as Rani of Jhansi, India's Warrior Queen. She was born in 1827 in Varanasi, a town in northern India. Indian society was highly patriarchal at that time. In 1842, at age fourteen, she was married to the middle-aged king, Raja Gangadhar Rao Niwalkar as his second wife. Unfortunately, even today, some parents prefer to marry off their daughters at such a young and delicate age. It is the age at which a girl flourishes and starts to dream about her life. The same happened with Rani. After marriage, she got her new name, "Lakshmi Bai." The young Lakshmi Bai gave birth to a son in 1851, but he died four months later. Later, she and Raja Gangadhar adopted the son of his cousin and named him Damodar Rao. Early marriage, the loss of her son, and all other injustices could not stop Rani from being a leader. With her vulnerability and strength, she became one of the leading personalities in the revolt of 1857 in India. To protect Jhansi from the attacks of the British army, she developed an army that included women. Though India was defeated in the first war of independence, Rani Laxmi Bai lit the fire of enthusiasm and courage in the people of India.[7]

Today, Rani Laxmi Bai of Jhansi is remembered as one of the greatest freedom fighters in Indian history. Movies, TV shows, books, and even nursery rhymes have kept her memory alive. Almost a century after she died in battle in 1858, the Indian National Army formed an all-female unit that helped the country in its war for independence in the 1940s. It was called the Rani of Jhansi regiment.

Although it is excellent to build monuments in remembrance of famous people, it is high time we valued the living as well. We have had such Ranis in every age. However, most of them do not get the credit due for their services to humanity.

---

7. Britannica. (2020). "Lakshmi Bai". Retrieved from: https://www.britannica.com/biography/Lakshmi-Bai.

Women are not new to leadership. Consider the example of powerhouse Angela Dorothea Merkel, who has served as chancellor of Germany since 2005. Merkel is one of the most powerful women in the world, as well as the *de facto* leader of the European Union. She has played a massive role in pulling Germany out of the 2008 financial crisis and steering it back to growth. *Forbes* ranked Merkel number one on its list of 100 Most Powerful Women for nine consecutive years.[8] This recognition is genuinely an incredible achievement, not only for Merkel but for all women.

Similarly, think about Jacinda Ardern of New Zealand, who was the youngest female head of state in the world when she became prime minister. She is also one of the few world leaders who gave birth to a child while in office. Impressive, isn't it? In the wake of the recent mass shooting in her country, Ardern showed a great sense of compassion. In this mass shooting, dozens of worshipers at two mosques were killed. To condemn this action, she wore a black hijab and grieved alongside victims' families. She also took prompt action to ban military-style semiautomatic weapons within days of the shooting. Empathy is like a sun that emits all moral qualities. And it takes strength to be an empathetic leader.

EMPATHY IS LIKE A SUN THAT
EMITS ALL MORAL QUALITIES.

What a fantastic leader Ardern is. When I read about such women, I feel proud that I belong to such a compassionate gender.

8. *Forbes*. (2019). "The World's 100 Most Powerful Women." Retrieved from: https://www.forbes.com/power-women/#25c8f27d5e25.

Apart from female political leaders, the world is full of successful female entrepreneurs, business leaders, engineers, scientists, and investors. However, things are still challenging for women in many parts of the world, especially for women of color.

You might be wondering what it means to be "a woman of color." The term "person of color" is generally—but not always—used to describe all the people who are not "white." For this book, we will stick to that definition.

LOOK AT LIMITS BUT TO PUSH THEM

A limit is defined by the fear that holds us back. That's why knowing those fears is essential to push our boundaries. While more women may be educated and employed today than ever before, the same old inequalities have simply followed us to new places. I recently read an article on the World Economic Forum's website that was quite disappointing, but necessary to know. According to the article, "It will be a staggering 208 years before the U.S. reaches gender parity."[9] How distressing. Meanwhile, the gains that have been made have not extended to all women equally. Women in our society, including women of color and LGBTQ+, women are still the most likely to be trapped in minimum-wage jobs. Even in the so-called advanced twenty-first century, women face discrimination and harassment in the workplace, ranging from the pay gap and gender biases to sexual assault.

In my efforts to understand gender inequity at work, I conducted several interviews looking at the personal barriers women face in finding their *why* in the workplace. They are discussed below.

---

9. World Economic Forum. "Accelerating gender parity in Globalization 4.0" Retrieved from: https://www.weforum.org/agenda/2019/06/accelerating-gender-gap-parity-equality-globalization-4/.

> A LIMIT IS DEFINED BY THE FEAR
> THAT HOLDS US BACK.

"What If" Phenomenon

Generally, women feel more self-doubt than men. Unfortunately, self-doubt hinders leadership. For women, the emotional hazards of leadership and speaking up are particularly high. What if they hate me? What if I do not fit? What if I cannot keep up? These are just some of the self-doubting thoughts that arise due to the fear of being critically judged. We women are conditioned to act in ways that ensure our likability. We have watched, or experienced, how women are shamed when they do anything that might be perceived as arrogant or "not nice." It is no wonder that our safety instinct and inner critic goes on high alert when we contemplate playing a more significant role in our work or lives.

Lack of Support

Another barrier is the lack of support. Today, people are generally more negative than positive. Pundits and men in power are very much interested in criticizing women when they try to break stereotypes. Very few will support you. If no one around you encourages your need for personal growth, it is enough to stop you from trying to grow. A lack of mentors and sponsors in the workplace or in their personal lives plays a significant role in holding women back.

Perfectionism

Perfectionism is a personality trait marked by high personal performance standards and an unnecessary desire to be flawless and perfect. This attribute leads to extremely critical self-evaluation and concerns regarding how others will judge us. Perfectionism hinders success for many women. They fear failure or being judged by society. Therefore, they set such unrealistic standards for themselves that they cannot achieve as much. Not working toward growth because you cannot do it perfectly is a common mistake. You end up feeling, "I am not suitable or ready to lead."

NOT WORKING TOWARD GROWTH BECAUSE
YOU CANNOT DO IT PERFECTLY IS A
COMMON MISTAKE.

Inflexibility

Many women, just like my mother, did not accept any promotions just because they did not want to compromise their responsibilities toward their family. This situation happens when workplaces do not allow flexible work schedules. Assuming a higher role may mean more time at work, which can take away time from families. As a woman, it can be a daunting balancing act. Therefore, many women give up in the middle of their careers, even if they have high potential.

Pay Gap

The pay gap is a dilemma for our society. Women of all races are paid less than men for the same work, and the difference only gets worse as a woman's career progresses. No matter how qualified you may be, it does not help if your employer does not provide pay and benefit incentives proportional to responsibilities required to fulfill the job requirements if you are a woman. It is quite demotivating, isn't it? You work hard and perform, but you get less compensation than your male coworker.

Gender pay gap data[10] clearly shows that men tend to earn more than women. When we compare all men to all women, regardless of industry, job type, years of experience, and so forth, women earn less than men. A gender pay gap is a metric that tells us the difference in pay between men and women. It's a measure of inequality and captures a concept that is broader than the idea of equal pay for equal work. In the past decades, the gap has reduced, but still, there remains a gap.

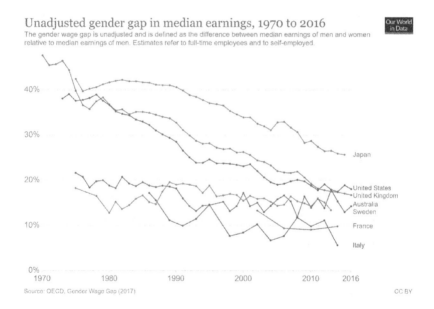

Unadjusted gender gap in median earnings, 1970 to 2016

The gender wage gap is unadjusted and is defined as the difference between median earnings of men and women relative to median earnings of men. Estimates refer to full-time employees and to self-employed.

Source: OECD, Gender Wage Gap (2017)

There is no simple answer to the question, "Why don't more women, especially women of color, find their *why* to go for leadership positions?" Despite the advantages of my background and experiences, I have countless times felt unsupported, invisible, and uncomfortable during my pursuit to develop and advance my

10. Our World in Data "Economic inequality by Gender." Retrieved from: https://ourworldin-data.org/economic-inequality-by-gender.

career. It is hard to strive for something when you doubt your "be-longing" and wonder if you are unfairly treated or overlooked. It is well-documented that women face a "double burden" of discrimination and stereotypes—this burden triples for women of color with the additional burden of hidden bias.

IT IS WELL-DOCUMENTED THAT WOMEN FACE A "DOUBLE BURDEN" OF DISCRIMINATION AND STEREOTYPES—THIS BURDEN TRIPLES FOR WOMEN OF COLOR WITH THE ADDITIONAL BURDEN OF HIDDEN BIAS.

As I continue to reflect more on my background and experiences, I realize many of the professional women of color I know are very capable of leadership. However, they were not always given the titles (CEO, president, director, etc.) we typically associate with leadership. They had the skills, but may have been overlooked, quietly doing the work of a leader without the recognition.

TAKEAWAYS

In short, finding a self-motivating *why* for leadership will remain an issue if women continue to lack the sense of "it feels right" compared to men as they rise through the ranks. These issues are driving many talented women either not to consider or to leave leadership positions. This situation stalls equal representation halfway up the corporate ladder. Looking at the above factors, I think we need to play a role in focusing energy on expanding women's power and influence. We can do it by positioning more women across the country to make decisions, shape perspectives, and control resources in their homes, workplaces, and communities. For that, we need to carefully examine the work experiences of women of color and the causes of women's underrepresentation in leadership roles, be it in business, politics, or other organizations.

SELF-REFLECTION EXERCISE:
FINDING YOUR WHY

Your story is a powerful tool toward finding your why. Use this worksheet to create a measure of impactful events starting from your early life:

1. Think of an important experience as a child that helped shape your journey toward your future.

    _____
    _____
    _____

2. List at least three women who have heavily influenced you.

    _____
    _____
    _____

3. List at least three opportunities that have had a life-changing effect on you.

    _____
    _____
    _____

4. What use of these experiences, people, and opportunities have you made till now?

    _____
    _____
    _____

5. Are you ready to be an influencer for women who want to lead?

    _____
    _____
    _____

CHAPTER 2

BREAKING THROUGH
YOUR CLOUDS

"The best protection any woman can have…is courage."

— Elizabeth Cady Stanton

What do you think is the most important trait of a successful woman?

Our answers might differ, but that is okay. Based on my years of work experience and education, I believe the most prominent attribute of a successful woman is her ability to speak up for herself. It is her courage and audacity that brings her to success.

How?

THE MOST PROMINENT ATTRIBUTE OF A
SUCCESSFUL WOMAN IS HER ABILITY TO
SPEAK UP FOR HERSELF.

Let me start with a true story.

Whenever I go to India to visit my parents, I get the opportunity to meet a lot of women. These simple yet strong women provoke me to ponder the bigger picture of equity. Most of the women I have seen growing up in India are very hard-working in whatever role they pursue. Their courage and enthusiasm inspire me. Frankly speaking, to me, the greatest influencers are not the women CEOs or leaders I admire in Seattle. They are the women and girls around me who are not afraid to talk about their dreams despite their profound obstacles. By no means am I degrading the female CEO or leader. They are inspirations for every woman and man in the world. However, it is extraordinary to see fearlessness to achieve great goals among women who may not have had the privileges of good education and opportunities to grow in life. I feel fearlessness with purpose is courage.

I FEEL FEARLESSNESS WITH PURPOSE IS COURAGE.

For me, one such influencer was a young girl named Kanchan. She was sixteen and came from an impoverished household in Delhi. My parents had hired her as daytime domestic help. She worked ten hours every day at my parents' home. Her duties included cooking, cleaning, and other household chores.

During the evening, she would walk almost four miles to a sewing class. Impressive, isn't it? After working for ten hours, you can imagine how drained one feels. Nonetheless, these powerhouse women are so hard-working because they must support their families. My mom told me that Kanchan had given up taking Sundays off and would come to work on weekends as well to earn extra money. I was amazed by her will to thrive and wondered where she got all the energy.

One day, at my parents' place. I was talking to someone on the phone in English. Kanchan was in the room, dusting furniture. During the entire conversation, she stared at me with an expression of amazement. Maybe she wondered what I was talking about during the call. When I hung up, Kanchan walked up to me, looked into my eyes, and said in Hindi, "I want to learn English."

"What?" I muttered. I was a little thrown by this because it was quite unexpected. I thought I had come to visit my parents, not be a tutor. However, I liked her confidence and enthusiasm, so I could not turn her down. I smiled and asked her in Hindi, "Have you completed your school?"

"Yes, but I don't know how to speak English," she answered with the same confidence. I nodded. She said, "I want to learn. Can you help me?"

I smiled and said, "Yes, I can."

I knew she was not convinced I would help. Over the day, she asked me several times if I would be able to teach her. Though I was not sure if I could manage to tutor her, I kept saying yes.

The next day, Kanchan's mother visited our house to drop off a few clothes she had altered for us. When I talked to her regarding Kanchan, she told me she was happy that her daughter had work to support herself. However, she was worried her daughter would have to live in poverty the way she had unless she could get a real job. She wanted her daughter to learn English because she thought it would help her get a good job.

It takes great courage to ask for what you want, especially when your workplace has quite a different role for you. Kanchan had a charming combination of bravery and self-esteem that allowed her to ask for an English tutor, even though she belonged to a poor household where women worked as domestic help to earn their livelihoods.

Kanchan did not have control over anyone. All she had was innocence that made her speak from her heart, saying, "Please help me flourish." She probably didn't even realize how bold she was, but we all, including her mother, knew it, and her mother did not ask her to be quiet. That is what matters the most. When we have someone who can support us in accomplishing our goals, our vision becomes clearer. Kanchan's mother was not educated, but she understood the importance of education and acquiring skills; she wanted her daughter to break the stereotype.

Kanchan's power to say it out loud guided her in the right direction. The unique strokes of your courage and skills paint your achievements. And that is the gist of this chapter. Not everyone can take on leadership and exercise power to change anything. However, everyone can learn and apply the methods and strategies demonstrated by the influencers around us.

THE UNIQUE STROKES OF YOUR COURAGE AND SKILLS PAINT YOUR ACHIEVEMENTS.

Before moving forward, let me complete Kanchan's story. When I realized how determined Kanchan was to learn English, I sat with her, and we developed a study plan. Her work schedule was quite tight, and she did not have much room to learn a new skill. Therefore, I introduced her to the concept of time management so she could fulfill her responsibilities and have room for self-growth. I enlightened her about the idea of taking a scheduled break to create room for self-care. I encouraged her to do basic things like reading English newspapers and magazines, and most importantly, have a conversation in English whenever and wherever possible, without any hesitation or shyness. With her determination and hard work, her family and her employers (my parents) understood what she was up to and happily agreed to support her. That is how her journey of learning English started. I helped Kanchan get the relevant books and practice papers. Now it was up to her to manage her time, and I must say, she did it efficiently.

Kanchan's brave step so much inspired the other girls in her community that they all began to follow her path. It was all triggered by just one young girl who dared to look into my eyes and say, "I want to learn English."

Do you know what made Kanchan so brave and fearless?

She was clear about her *why*. She knew that learning English was an important step toward landing a better job. Moreover, she did not feel ashamed when she asked me if I would help her. Often, we are truly clear about our goals and dreams, but we cannot pursue them because we are afraid to speak up. We are so scared of failure or rejection, which is why we don't ask. Albert Einstein said, *"The important thing is never to stop questioning."*

When I came back from my visit to India, I had developed a great sense of empowerment. Kanchan's motivation to learn English made me look at life from another perspective—the problem-solving perspective. I started awakening to a bigger picture. I decided to join conversations and communities related to women's empowerment. My purpose was to know what the future held, especially for women of color. By then, the term "feminism" had become quite common. Every other person would talk about feminism, but very few knew the true essence of it. Many people still think feminism is an aggressive movement, and it is all about proving that women are better than men. This notion is not correct. Feminism is not a movement; it is a theory. It is not a competition between the two genders to prove who is better. Instead, it is a struggle for equal treatment. It is not a new concept or trend; in the United States, feminism's "first wave" really began at the Seneca Falls Convention in 1848. It is impossible to fathom the future if I don't glance at the past

OCEAN OF SUFFRAGE AND ITS WAVES OF FEMINISM

As I write this book, we are marking the hundredth anniversary of the Nineteenth Amendment's passage, giving women the constitutional right to vote. This year of 2020 is a historic centennial. We are fortunate to be able to commemorate it an important milestone of democracy and can explore its relevance to equal rights issues.

Women's suffrage means the right of women to vote in elections. At the beginning of the mid-nineteenth century, women worked for economic and political equality, and for social reforms. They sought to change voting laws to allow them to vote. In the early twentieth century, feminist activity in the English-speaking world that tried to win women's suffrage ignited a new surge of feminism.

Did you know there were four waves of feminism?[11]

The First Wave (before 1848–1920)

Although it is not celebrated common knowledge like it should be, women in the nineteenth and early twentieth centuries knew they must first gain political power (including the right to vote) if

---

11. Martha Rampton, Pacific University Oregon. "Four Waves of Feminism." Retrieved from: https://www.pacificu.edu/magazine/four-waves-feminism.

they were to bring about change. They used that understanding to fuel the fire leading to the theory of feminism. Their agenda also expanded to issues concerning sexual, reproductive, and economic matters. The wave planted a seed of belief that women had the potential to contribute just as much as men.

The Second Wave (the 1960s–1980s)

This wave gained momentum in the context of the anti-war and civil rights movements. The voice of the wave was increasingly radical with the rising new left. In this phase, workplace, sexuality, and reproductive rights were important issues. The focus was also on women to meet their equality goals regardless of sex under the Equal Rights Amendment or ERA (which has still not been ratified).

The Third Wave (the 1990s–early 2000s)

Unlike the earlier feminist movements, the term "feminist" was less well received by the female population during the third wave due to varying feminist outlooks. This was in response to the second wave's perceived failures and the backlash against second-wave initiatives. This wave challenged the definitions of femininity that grew out of the second wave's ideas, arguing that the second-wave over-emphasized experiences of upper-middle-class white women. The third wave saw women's lives with an angle of *intersectionality*. It is the categorization to demonstrate a connection of how race, class, backgrounds, faith, religious beliefs, gender, and origins are all significant factors when discussing feminism. It examined issues related to women's lives anywhere around the world. The fight continued to vanquish disparities in male and female pay and protect women's reproductive rights. Pursuits continued to end violence against women in our nation as well as abroad. This wave was about acceptance and a real understanding of the term feminism.

Much progress has been made since the dawn of the first wave; much is still left to be done. The feminist issues today are wide-ranged, so it is much harder to label what feminism is.

The Fourth Wave (2012–present)

The fourth wave of feminism began earlier in the second decade of the twenty-first century, and it continues today. It is quite like the third wave. However, its focus is on sexual harassment, body shaming, and rape culture.

In the current century, things have improved a great deal. Women of color have entered the workforce in large numbers. However, they still face systemic barriers when it comes to promotion and growth. The battle is far from over, and we need to fight it until sexist bias is eliminated from the workplace. Where do we start as women of color to get our place on top?

CULTIVATING BEHAVIOR TO SOW CHANGE:
WAVE WITHIN

Big changes do not happen overnight. We can always start with small steps. One such step is writing this book. I want to share awareness, stories, and ideas to cultivate positive change for women of color who are trying to succeed and willing to break the mold of inequity. After interviewing a diverse set of women, I put together a list of behaviors and actions I find vital for creating positive change.

Embrace Failures Equally

Success is a good thing to enjoy and keep us motivated. But what happens when we fail? Do we stop there? One thing to learn from failure is that it is going to be temporary if we keep trying. Once we learn that, it's easier to realize that failures usually drive us to leave our comfort zone and work for change. This behavior to use the benefit from the failure is helpful, maybe even necessary, for keeping us motivated in our endeavors to rise. But if they do not lead to action, they are not going to help a positive change.

Many of us are so plagued with losing that we don't want to revisit failures. It's the fear of failure that takes your dream away, not the failure. However, looking back at failures provides valuable insight. It's when we focus solely on failure that we run into trouble.

IT'S THE FEAR OF FAILURE THAT TAKES
YOUR DREAM AWAY, NOT THE FAILURE.

Furthermore, when things are not going well, forcing yourself to give up can cause more damage. You cannot eliminate all the negativity from your life. You must learn how to survive with the negativity around you—find the balance between acknowledging the negative and striving for the positive. Sometimes, you must stay stuck in the situation, no matter how difficult it is. Persistent pursuit is where the real challenge is.

A difference exists between women who want to lead and women who are leading. Leaders are those who, instead of avoiding challenges, have tried harder during challenges. These women have proved that when it comes to making changes, the main ingredient is their *skill*. Mental blocks shouldn't blur your skills. Don't be tormented by unexpected outcomes; instead, keep your skills sharp and focus on your abilities.

Make Every Effort to Overcome

We all have challenges we need to overcome. So instead of pleading to give up and move on, we should look around for examples of women who have found solutions to the problems we face every day.

This book is not meant to verbally persuade you to change the behaviors that may restrict your leadership potential. I know it would be wonderful if we could eliminate barring behaviors with just a few words. It has been tried many times over the generations, but verbal volleys alone cannot always produce change. For example, if you are very conscious about body image and constantly fighting with weight, wouldn't it be nice just to set reminders on your phone to keep you on track with your diet and be done with it? However, we all know losing weight is an uphill battle, so changing our behaviors requires much more than verbal or written coaxing. We need to facilitate gentle insights—they succeed where forceful persuasion fails.

WE NEED TO FACILITATE GENTLE INSIGHTS—THEY SUCCEED WHERE FORCEFUL PERSUASION FAILS.

Let me give you a real-world example of how changes start at a personal level. Let's analyze the issue of the maternal wall.

We all know how successful women may suddenly face being stereotyped once they enter maternity. Joan C. Williams, professor of law and author, conceived the phrase "maternal wall." It cautions that "women who have been very successful may suddenly find their proficiency questioned once they become pregnant, take maternity leave, or adopt flexible work schedules."[12]

This bias that working mothers encounter undermines the advancement of their careers, and their competency gets questioned. An increasing percentage of the wage gap between men and women is attributable to the maternal wall. Plenty of evidence-based research is available to address this obstacle in the middle of a woman's career. Women are often stereotyped after motherhood. But two women, Lauren and Lindsay, decided to address the situation and search for a workable strategy to tear down the maternal wall in the workplace. They cofounded the Returnity Project. They built a community platform supporting thousands of women to share their return to work stories after maternity leave. The Returnity Project not only focuses on sharing real stories but also provides resources. In summer 2019, Returnity Kits were launched to give women (and men) returning to work from maternity leave even more support. The kits include products and community resources for working mothers. The kits are a meaningful evolution in the Returnity Project's mission.

When Lauren and Lindsay met for the first time, they were both pregnant. After returning to work, they proudly mastered career and motherhood balance and wanted to help others do the same. They are always expanding their list of needed changes in workplaces, like gender dynamics and career opportunities, to continue to support women who want to work and raise families.[13] The purpose of sharing their example is to explain that barriers like the maternal

---

12. Joan C. Willams (2004). "The Maternal Wall." *Harvard Business Review*. Retrieved from: https://hbr.org/2004/10/the-maternal-wall.

13. The Riveter, New Mothers Need More Support When They Return to Work. Period. Retrieved from: https://theriveter.co/voice/new-mothers-need-more-support-when-they-return-to-work-period/

wall can also become a point on which to connect and something to overcome together. We can't make big changes alone, but we can add up our efforts and form a bigger solution.

Cutting Off Coping

It's usually easier to cope with a situation than accept the challenge of changing it. We women are good at discovering or inventing methods to deal with hardship. Women are more likely to shed stress by talking to a friend or a close family member. They are not necessarily looking for solutions but may just want to engage with a person close to them.

LEARNING HOW TO COPE WITH A PROBLEM CAN BE A BIGGER PROBLEM THAN THE PROBLEM ITSELF.

Learning how to cope with a problem can be a bigger problem than the problem itself. A lack of action on what caused the issue can lead to a downward spiral. It can leave women facing even more challenges when breaking into leadership. Of course, it is vital to be able to handle failures, but our character is revealed in how we handle them. Consider the example of Stacey Abrams. She was the first black woman in the history of the United States to be nominated by the Democratic party for governor. Despite her extraordinary efforts for the public, which earned her several high-profile endorsements, including one from former President Obama, she lost. However, her fighting spirit never accepted defeat. Instead, she challenged the results. Her opponent, Brian Kemp, was also serving as Georgia's Secretary of State, which meant he was overseeing the election he was running in. Abrams' position was that Kemp had a conflict of interest and used his office to suppress voting. She highlighted evidence of voter purges and blocked registration processing, leaving a massive number of voter registrations pending before elections, which led to unfair results. In 2019, Abrams announced the founding of Fair Fight 2020, an organization aimed at assisting Democrats financially and technically in building voter protection teams in twenty states.

Abrams is Fair Fight Action 2020's chairperson. Abrams is an excellent example of a woman who is not afraid to fight for change even while facing defeat. She does not hesitate to question any injustice she witnesses. She is a product of her choice, not her circumstances. Her reaction to the situation shows every woman the power to change the situation by responding with the right attitude.

The critical insight here is to be truthful with yourself about the extent of your aspiration. Once you know what you want, then fight for it whole-heartedly. Don't count your punches but make your spirit count.

I have grown from many setbacks. It's vital as a woman not to push yourself back with failures. The reason many women fear losses is they get labeled easily. They are told it's their fault. Therefore, I stress the importance of reaping the benefit even by making mistakes. That benefit appears in the form of wisdom and understanding. Also, let's not miss out on opportunities to learn from the failures of others. Respect every failure as your teacher.

ANY CRACK IN YOUR DREAM DOES NOT MEAN IT'S SHATTERED AND YOU CAN'T FIX IT.

Any crack in your dream does not mean it's shattered and you can't fix it. Those who know what they want and why they want it are the ones who keep the bubble of persistence around. They don't allow themselves to break. Trust your determination; it's your compass toward your goals.

The fire inside us to succeed must never be put out with sprinkles of disappointments. Your dreams are your commitments to yourself to achieve what you honestly desire. Don't let go of those aspirations that excite you, prompt you, and make you come back. Endurance is the platform, and strength is the pillar. Together they hold your success.

Burning Off the Burnout

I have been guilty of focusing on work as if it is "all that matters." Women sometimes get so absorbed in doing their best that they forget to figure out the purpose behind it. This problem becomes more complicated if you are a person of color. It is much easier for us to bury our heads and focus on tangible results. Because there aren't many who look like us, our conversations in the workplace are often limited to only formal encounters. There are not many informal conversations or casual talks that allow people to have a better perception of each other's personalities. This isolation is significant when people are trying to review your performance or work.

Many female leaders agree that building relationships at work, in addition to excellent performance, is the key to success. Many female leaders agree that to be successful, building relationships at work is just as important as excellent performance. I will cite the example of Carla Harris, vice chairman, managing director, and senior client advisor at Morgan Stanley. Harris is one of the highest-ranking African-American women on Wall Street. She has shared the lessons she learned along her way in her two books, *Strategize to Win* and *Expect to Win*. She coined the term "performance currency," which means women over-invest in getting great results and ignore "relationship currency," which is investing time to connect with peers at work. According to Harris, women value performance currency more because of the clear concept of "hard work = success."

Still, relationship currency can seem vague because you can't see the connection to success. She says building relationships should be an intentional act, even for women who do not have this natural inclination.

> IT IS FRUITFUL TO INTENTIONALLY INVEST
> IN RELATIONSHIPS IN THE WORKPLACE.

If you don't have supportive relationships at work, you don't know whom to reach out to when you need help. Then you face isolation and less access to information necessary to perform well. My takeaway from her lesson is to make sure you don't underestimate the importance of building relationships. It is vital to use every nugget of time you can get, be it walking to Starbucks or taking a rest break together. It is fruitful to intentionally invest in relationships in the workplace. Also, be sure to utilize relationships positively to get the support and feedback you need to advance.

De-Normalizing the Normal

Whenever I interview women, I consider them experts in their own lives. I get the view that, despite noticeable gender inequity issues, women are fine with how things are at work. The Riveter, an organization devoted to a gender-equal coworking space, along with partners Xerox and YouGov, surveyed a representative sample of 1,550 women across racial groups, professions, and caregiving roles to statistically explore their daily experiences. According to the report, *Workforce for Change*, women are well aware of how gender, race, body shape, and caregiving roles influenced their work and advancement opportunities. Women know the price they pay daily—what they sacrifice to get through the rocky road of inequity in the workplace. The report calls it "normalization of inequity" and concludes that the divide it creates among women may be one of the biggest hurdles to overcome.[14]

Racial and women's issues are not separate. Yes, few women of color have attained leadership positions despite all odds, but I want people to understand these are exceptions, not the standard. The women who have made it into C-suite offices are far outnumbered by men who have worked in the same environment and climbed the ladder quickly. We need to understand how modern workplaces have changed in appearance. I say: Don't keep looking for normal—it conceals the beauty of diversity.

DON'T KEEP LOOKING FOR NORMAL—
IT CONCEALS THE BEAUTY OF DIVERSITY.

The baggage of bias pulls women of color behind. Most women of color just deal with it rather than confront the weight of it. Most women are aware that appearance is one of many aspects controlling

---

14. The Riveter. "A Work Force for Change: Driving equity in the workplace and beyond." November 2019.

their professional experience, and they just internalize it. Appearance overlaps with issues of ageism, body types, disability, and ethnicity. Women, when subjected continuously to these biases, mostly give up trying to fight embedded unfair treatment.

These hidden biases are hard to tackle. They are limiting opportunities, leading to invisibility, and camouflaging the work women have done. We need to stop considering this behavior normal and identify and confront the status quo rather than navigating it.

Let's Not Take Less

A quick flashback to Chapter 1—women are paid less than men on average. According to the 2017 US Census Bureau data, the average gender pay gap in the United States is around 19.5 percent, meaning that, on average, a woman earns 80.5 percent of what her male counterpart does. On average, it takes an additional forty-four days for a woman to make the same annual salary as her male counterparts. The pay gap widens for older females if we narrow the data to age ranges. Despite the Equal Pay Act of 1963, employers do seem to be conforming to the rules.

> ON AVERAGE, IT TAKES AN ADDITIONAL FORTY-FOUR DAYS FOR A WOMAN TO MAKE THE SAME ANNUAL SALARY AS HER MALE COUNTERPARTS.

The issue of less pay is not entirely about employers' will. It can be a sum of choices, opportunities, recognition, mentorship, performance, perceptions, and professional development, which a woman can get during her career. The *Workforce for Change Report* by Riveter talks about two major contributing factors in the wage gap—lack of promotions and lack of negotiation.

I'm in the healthcare industry, which is heavily saturated with female employees. I wanted to see if the high number of females contributed to better outcomes regarding the pay gap. Using many credible sources, I was amazed to find the pay gap still exists. Bureau of Labor Statistics (BLS) data[15] shows that in every sector, women's earnings are much lower than those of their male counterparts. This is even true for industries where women outnumber men.

Source: U.S. Bureau of Labor Statistics, Current Population Survey.

This finding is sad for me because it proves the issue of equity may not be just related to the lack of inclusion. Although women make up the majority of the healthcare workforce, they hold only a small percentage of hospital C-level positions, and they head only a minute percentage of healthcare companies. Women have outnumbered men in healthcare for years, yet they have not moved into

15. Bureau of Labor and Statistics. "Highlights of Women's earnings in 2018". Retrieved from: https://www.bls.gov/opub/reports/womens-earnings/2018/home.htm.

positions of prominence and power in proportion to their numbers in the workforce.[16]

Why are women not entering leadership as often? According to the women I surveyed, part of the problem is that women do not play a role in strategic planning or operations in many organizations. Hence, women lack visibility when it comes to opportunities in these roles. Many women of color reported having never received a promotion or even being considered for one. And if a woman does get promoted, she may be so thankful for the consideration that she does not negotiate compensation. According to a workforce for change report by Riveter, 71 percent of women do not negotiate their pay.

> 71 PERCENT OF WOMEN DO NOT NEGOTIATE THEIR PAY.

The First Step

It's time to take a fresh look at the old glass ceiling. Women's ability to negotiate for advancement and pay both need attention and require meaningful conversations in work cultures. But first, let's look at current trends reflected in the Bureau of Labor Statistics report, Women in the Labor Force: a Databook.

According to this report, Women held 50.04 percent of American jobs as of December 2019. The number of women en-

---

16. Our World in Data. "Representation of women in senior managerial positions." Retrieved from: https://ourworldindata.org/economic-inequality-by-gender.

tering the workforce has increased, but in my opinion, workforce participation does not indicate a real scenario of equity.

You must be wondering why is that?

Despite more women in the workforce, there is an over-representation of women in low-paying occupations. Women in senior and middle management positions in the US and around the world are underrepresented in high-profile, better-paying jobs. Women require greater work flexibility due to their expected gender roles, and the following data verifies it.

- Demographically, labor force participation varies by marital status and differs between women. Never-married women had the highest participation rate of all women at 64.5 percent in 2018. Separated and divorced women were more likely to be employed than married women (58.2 percent). By contrast, married men were more likely to participate in the labor force.

- Workforce numbers for women with children under 18 years of age was 71.4 percent in March 2018. The labor force participation rate for those with children 6 to 17 years old was higher than for those with younger children. Unmarried mothers are more likely to participate in the labor force than married mothers.

- Women are more likely to work part-time. Twenty-four percent of employed women usually worked part-time—that is, less than thirty-five hours per week in 2018 in comparison to men at 12 percent. The percentage of employed women working part-time has not changed much over the past five decades.

- Foreign-born women were less likely than native-born women to be in the labor force in 2018. By contrast, foreign-born men were more likely to be in the labor force than were native-born men.

The trends above are precisely what I experienced as a working immigrant mother. There may be an added cultural expectation, but I feel, in general, care issues affect most of the women. The responsibility of care and cost of care are compelling factors. More women have been forced to choose more flexible work, which may be part-time and closer to home because they mainly provide care for their families. The increased burden of the high cost of childcare can aggravate the situation. I felt stretched too thin to cover ten weeks of lengthy summer vacations of school. The 9 a.m. to 4 p.m. times of school affected the potential to work full time without relying on backup care.

Further research is needed to analyze women's experiences in the workforce as the fight for gender parity continues. If we view climbing the corporate ladder as a step-by-step process, the first step on the ladder will be the trickiest, since it is a challenge for women. When it comes to hiring for a managerial position, fewer women feel supported to take on the role. Overall, the C-suite offices have recently gained more feminine presence. Still, less than 8 percent of C-suite executives are women. And only three out of thirty-eight C-suite executives are women of color in the year 2020.

TAKEAWAYS

The various statistics, studies, and examples shared in this chapter paint a picture of lack when it comes to leadership roles for women of color. Nevertheless, the goal is not to focus on negatives but to diagnose the situation correctly. When we draw a roadmap to the executive level, we find women are detoured from the beginning. Women need the opportunity to take that first step. Women climbing up need to extend one hand back down the ladder, becoming mentors who help other women follow. If you are way up the ladder, then work to make that first rung available to women.

Women in power have the potential to shatter the already cracking ceiling. In the next chapter, I will talk in-depth about the behaviors and examples that support this change and revolutionize the process by which women rise to leadership positions, giving the process a much-awaited boost. People choose behaviors depending on the results of their or others' actions. Therefore, let's tap into today's leaders' experiences and share them to spread the success to all women.

SELF-REFLECTION EXERCISE:
BREAKING THROUGH YOUR CLOUDS

1. Define your comfort zone and list the skills that come easily to you.

   _____

   _____

   _____

2. Now think of the skills that you desire for your advancement or success.

   _____

   _____

   _____

   _____

3. What is stopping you from gaining the skills you desire?

   _____

   _____

   _____

   _____

4. What can you do to remove the barriers to acquire new skills?

   _____

   _____

   _____

   _____

5. Commit yourself to a plan to learn and master the skills you aspire to achieve.

   _____

   _____

   _____

CHAPTER 3

REACHING YOUR SKY

"A truly equal world would be one where women ran half our countries and companies and men ran half our homes."

— **Sheryl Sandberg**

In the previous chapter, I introduced the idea of the how—women are missing at lower-level management positions, thus blocking them from the leadership ladder altogether. Just suppose you are running an obstacle course. To win, you must move through the obstacles as quickly as you can. However, the course's starting line is blocked by a pile of massive rocks. How can you navigate the course if you can't get onto it? This is what the first step looks like for women when they attempt to step up in their organization or business.

Research shows that it is quite a daunting task for a woman to get past this initial hurdle and reach the managerial or senior level. However, many women in the world have successfully done so or have launched their own small businesses or non-profit organizations. The examples of high-powered women can help us to understand how they have achieved their success and mental fortitude.

Let's look at Danielle Shoots, vice president of business operations for Comcast's western division. Shoots is the youngest vice president in Comcast Cable Corporation's history. The most exciting part is that she did this in less than three years with the company and within the industry. Before Comcast, Danielle was the CFO for the largest division at the Colorado Department of Public Health and Environment. She was promoted to this role within one year of starting at the agency. She was just twenty-six at that time, making her the youngest CFO in the department's history and Denver's. In 2017, Danielle was named to the *Denver Business Journal*'s Forty under Forty business leaders.

THOUGH THE SKILLS LEARNED FROM PERSONAL EX-PERIENCES ARE NOT RESUME STUFF, THEY PLAY A CRUCIAL ROLE IN LEADERSHIP.

In her interviews and talks, Danielle has highlighted the value of women's personal experiences like marriage, motherhood, etc. According to her, such experiences are assets to women in their professional lives. Though the skills learned from personal experiences are not resume stuff, they play a crucial role in leadership. In her feature talk, Shoots said, "You have the tools already to get where you're going because you multi-task; because you walk into environments and have to look different than everybody in a room and somehow still get your voice heard; because you understand how to lead when nobody thinks you're going to do it right. That's magic. That's the stuff they don't tell us to tap into."[17]

---

17. The Riveter. "The 9 Leadership Tools Every Woman Needs to Know." Anderson, N. (2020). Retrieved from: https://theriveter.co/voice/the-leadership-tools-every-woman-needs-to-know-danielle-shoots-the-riveter-denver/.

Life experiences teach women survival skills, negotiation skills, interpersonal communication, etc., but workplaces have to play their part when it comes to promoting women.

Can workplaces learn from women's personal experiences?

To answer this question, I have a personal story to share.

When I became director of the rehab unit for the first time, my second child, Vansh, was only nine months old. I had an opportunity to step up from my clinic-based career. For me, the biggest challenge was not being a leader and a mother simultaneously. It was operating in a workplace not designed for working mothers. Even with the most supportive employer and coworkers, it was difficult.

One main issue was finding a place to use a breast pump. The facility was large and even had a designated smoking area, but there was no private space for females to attend to personal needs. That was a frustrating discovery.

Although the healthcare industry is saturated with females, workplaces and employers lack the basic support systems women need, especially post-maternity. I was a bit embarrassed to ask for help with this issue. The situation made me understand the challenges for young working mothers.

The notion that women with young kids should leave their "personal stuff" at home is ridiculous and unhealthy. Gender, motherhood, marriage, and ethnicity can all be overlapping circles, and the road to success can only be constructed if employers strive to provide a positive balance between personal and professional needs.

I know *the struggle* to achieve work, and home balance is universal, regardless of gender. However, it affects women more often than men, especially ethnic women. The imbalance is caused by ingrained gender roles and cultural biases and reinforced by unhelpful workplace structures.

I had to use my short-term disability, paid vacation time, and some unpaid time to cover my maternity leave during the birth of my kids, Krish and Vansh, in the United States. However, not every woman I knew had that option. Many of them opted out of work because the cost of daycare and lack of flexibility at work limited their choices. I don't mean to say the situation is entirely messed up. Trends are improving, with more women being able to return to work with better benefits and options. For example, in some organizations, women are allowed to work from home or have flexible working hours. However, on average, the return to work is still a steep slope for women.

Employers have an incentive to accommodate women's needs, as studies confirm the value of gender diversity in the workplace with clear statistical data highlighting the benefits on many levels, such as business, social, and employee satisfaction.

SO, HOW DO WE MAKE CHANGE INEVITABLE FOR WORKPLACES?

Changes in behavior are the sum of many micro-changes that lead to real change. Understanding these micro-changes requires introspection and action, which comes from inside and out. Once you have identified the behaviors that were stopping you from bringing positive change, you become an independent influence, convincing others to become part of that change. The following is a compilation of some highlights from my interviews about simple actions that can *ignite* a necessary change within and around you.

Learning to Be Yourself—No Matter How Different You May Be

If you stand out due to your skin color, mannerisms, and accents, does it make you self-conscious? A person raised in unique cultures far removed from mainstream America may have unique pronunciation. Many immigrant women strongly believe that an accent changes people's perception of what is being said and its credibility. Particularly strong accents appear to be incredibly challenging. Women fear their heavy accents will lead people to doubt their qualifications even more. An accent can cause the perception that the woman may not understand common cultural and business ethics or practices "here"—wherever here may be.

Cultural, awareness is a two-way street. Cultural acceptance's primary goal is not integration but respecting differences. In the United States, I feel most native speakers of English do not care about your accent as long as your meaning is clear. Women from diverse backgrounds must share their stories to help other women overcome their fears and lack of confidence. I have come to realize if we open up to people, most of them can relate to us.

EVEN WHEN PEOPLE HAVE DIFFERENT ORIGINS, STORIES BRING THEM TOGETHER.

Even when people have different origins, stories bring them together. When you are yourself, you allow others to create meaningful connections. When you form stronger bonds with your team or population, you serve as a leader.

I recently had an opportunity to speak to a trailblazing leader in Washington State, Manka Dhingra. She represents the forty-fifth legislative district in Washington State as a state senator. She became well known as the first Sikh elected to any state legislature in the United States. For me, she is an icon for women of color in leadership in Washington State.

Dhingra shared an interesting story regarding her oath ceremony, which helped me understand the importance of spreading cultural awareness. Before narrating her story, let me tell you she was born in Bhopal, India. A few years later, she and her family migrated to the United States (1986-87). She went on to graduate from the University of California, Berkeley, earning a Bachelor of Arts degree in history and political science. She later earned a degree from the University of Washington, School of Law in 1999.

During her oath ceremony for the state assembly, Sikh sacred music was played to welcome her to the state legislator. Dhingra told me that standing in the state senate while hearing the music and being with her family and peers as she took the oath was a significant moment to celebrate her life and culture. When I listened to her story, I was so overwhelmed. Dhingra shares this story with pride to inspire women from diverse backgrounds.

THE STRENGTH OF A SOCIETY LIES IN CELEBRATING CONTRASTS, NOT IN SEEKING SIMILARITIES.

Workplace cultures are increasingly coming to understand that the world is smaller than ever, so we must make meaningful changes that benefit everyone. The systems of the world—its governments, economies, religions, and cultures—are increasingly interdependent. The strength of a society lies in celebrating contrasts, not in seeking similarities.

Your Visibility Is as Vital as Your Eligibility

The facts say that men will apply for jobs when they meet only 60 percent of the requirements. However, women will only apply if they meet 100 percent of the company's needs.

I want to cite a survey by Tara Sophia Mohr,[18] which she conducted to dig deeper into this situation. She surveyed over 1,000 men and women, mostly American professionals, and got eye-opening responses. The top reason for women not to apply for the job was their perception that they did not meet the listed qualification and did not want to waste their time and energy.

> WOMEN FEAR THEIR FAILURES CAN MAKE THE BIAS EVEN STRONGER AND WILL CHALLENGE THEIR PROFESSIONALISM.

For them, the cost of applying was the risk of failure rather than wanting to avoid wasting their efforts. I relate well with this "fear." There is no room for failure for women because it sticks with them longer and is not easily forgotten. Women fear their failures can make the bias even stronger and will challenge their professionalism.

18. Mohr, T. (2014). "Why Women Don't Apply for Jobs Unless They're 100 Percent Qualified." *Harvard Business Review.* Retrieved from: https://hbr.org/2014/08/why-women-dont-apply-for-jobs-unless-theyre-100-qualified.

But why are women strict with application rules when considering advancement opportunities? There are three possible reasons:

- Firstly, it can be related to gender bias associated with the assessment of job performance. It has been commonly found that men are often hired or promoted based on their potential. By comparison, women are hired for their experience and track record. If women have seen that in other workplaces, it makes perfect sense they'd be less likely to apply for a job where they didn't meet the requirements.

- Secondly, girls are conditioned from a young age to follow the rules; they are rewarded in every aspect of their lives for being a "good girl." It also hints at how girls have greater success in school than boys. The higher achievement can be attributed to their better rule-following. But when it comes to applying for jobs in their career, this habit of adhering to requirements by the book can lead to narrowing down of opportunities for them.

- Thirdly, certifications and degrees have historically played a different role for women compared to men. The twentieth century saw women break into professional life—but only if they had the right training and the proper accreditations. The qualifications women earned were the only tags that could get women into the good ol' boys club. The history of following rules and ensuring qualifications are met fully also indicated women's belief in meritocracy. But unfortunately, workplaces, be they business or professional, are not entirely based on equal opportunities. This belief can result in overstressing on fulfilling every qualification and underusing advocacy and networking.

So, what can be done to maximize chances for women to be hired and promoted?

Per popular trends, most workplaces have been known to promote men based on potential and women based on experience. Workplaces need to check their trends and encourage women who have similar credentials but are less likely to apply. Women must equally watch out to break the mold of conditioning they receive from childhood about following every rule laid out without questioning. Their conditioning may cost them opportunities because they may take eligibility too literally. Finally, women should not just get sucked up in the race of gaining all the qualifications and underestimate the value of making valuable connections, which can be crucial for advancement and visibility. It is essential to acquire and keep your skills sharp, but it's equally important to keep healthy confidence in applying for advancement based on believing in yourself rather than just the criteria.

Let People Help You

Many women in leadership roles have experienced an enormous commitment of time, which can take a toll on their work-life balance. Real success depends on a leader's ability to be in control, collaborate, call for help, and ensure that call is answered sustainably. A great example of this collaborative behavior is Meera Satpathy, a compassionate leader from the non-profit world.

Meera's non-profit journey started twenty-two years ago. By the year 1998, Meera was a successful businesswoman. Although India was undergoing rapid economic reform with rapid privatization, she was thinking differently. Her empathetic heart could not ignore the challenges people face, specifically mothers, children, and adolescents. She was moved by the suffering of people living in the slums around the city, who lacked access to primary healthcare services. She was deeply disturbed about the life-threatening conditions they faced daily. Rapid urbanization in big cities aggravated the problem by marginalizing economically deprived people. She stepped up to take on the key fundamental issues of Human Development, long before the declaration of UN Millennium Development Goals in 2000. The non-profit organization Sukarya was born, with the purpose to reduce the infant mortality rate; improve maternal and child health, nutrition, and gender equality; and to empower women.

In Meera's own words, there were obstacles and challenges along the way, but she was determined to help people significantly impacted by an unequal society.

Sukarya is involved at the grassroots, having served more than 6 million people living in more than 600 villages and 100 slums in Delhi and Haryana, India. The organization continues to reach out to communities to provide accessible, excellent quality health services. It all could happen under Meera's strategic guidance.

In an interview with me, Meera mentioned that initially, many people in her close circle, including her friends and family thought she was experimenting with another start-up. They believed that she would give up after a while. She wasn't taken seriously at all. She didn't get much support right from the beginning, but she harnessed what she had. She did not turn down any help she could get despite being doubted by the closest of people for her pursuits of running a non-profit. She expressed that problems related to development issues are closely interconnected, so non-profits must integrate the full picture to offer their support. This vision is precisely seen in the way she designed most of Sukarya's interventions. She strongly feels that development and desirable results cannot be achieved alone. Everybody must play a crucial role—government, civil societies, foundations, corporations, community stakeholders, and other influential persons. It requires a collaborative approach and collective efforts to yield more significant results.

Meera's foresight and unhesitant approach to reach out separates her from the rest of social entrepreneurs and makes her extraordinary. As a leader, she has a noticeably clear and deliberate approach.

"It's hard to run your own non-profit, and fight bias against people who don't invest faith within the women-led organizations. It's like changing the wheels of the car while driving it."

She adds, "We grew up in a society where every girl is told that 'You are a girl; this is for your good, you should do this, and you should not do that.'" She reports that it's time for society as a whole to address both conscious and so-called "unconscious" biases that affect the funding, supporting, mentoring, and overall treatment of women, especially in non-profits. These steps toward equity cannot be limited to anti-bias awareness, which is necessary but insufficient. Peer support does not take place by luck; it must be intentionally structured and planned. Peer support should be understood as a supplement to, not a substitute for, your efforts. She said, "I had to work extra hard to win the support of my peers and even my family for this selfless cause, and much harder to have access to funds." This culture needs to change.

Meera's mantra to get support was to give the power back to her focus group, women, and children, in reforming society. She worked toward creating an environment to bring the focus rather than just asking to change it. Due to Meera's persistence, today, Sukarya is not merely a developmental organization focusing on health, but an empowerment organization that raises awareness. It gives people the tools to enable them to demand better services and be able to undertake simple methods to improve their wellbeing, thereby building a better society. Meera also founded Sukarya USA (a Seattle-based non-profit to support the programs of Sukarya in India) and continues to grow her organization globally.

Meera's story is a real success story of a woman's passion, enthusiasm, and determination. And most importantly, she is a woman ready to reach out and ask for the change she wants to see.

Genuine Inspiration Is the Best Qualification

Can genuine inspiration help women to step up?

Yes, it can. It took me a while to understand that performing my job diligently and doing high-quality work I had learned in training were not even the basic ingredients. I needed visibility to stand distinctly at my workplace. Advancement was more about who had built the right relationships and dared to propose big plans.

When it comes to rising to lead, women need to push past the margins and create their own space.

> WHEN IT COMES TO RISING TO LEAD,
> WOMEN NEED TO PUSH PAST THE MARGINS
> AND CREATE THEIR OWN SPACE.

I am sure most of us have heard about or seen the groundbreaking documentary, *Knock Down the House*, which tracks four women who ran for Congress in 2018. This documentary truly highlights how genuine inspiration can help us rise to the first rung and well beyond.

Rachel Lears, director of this exuberant documentary film, reached out to organizations such as Brand-New Congress and

Justice Democrats to find "charismatic female candidates who weren't career politicians but were called to represent their communities." The search led her to four female candidates:

- Alexandria Ocasio-Cortez was a waitress and bartender from New York who was worked double shifts to save her family home from foreclosure.

- Amy Vilela is a Nevada mom who lost her twenty-two-year-old daughter to a blood clot due to a lack of health insurance.

- Cori Bush is from St. Louis. She is the nurse who rushed to help the wounded during the Ferguson, Missouri, riots. She watched as the police shooting of an unarmed black man shook her community to its core.

- Paula Jean Swearengin is a coal miner's daughter from West Virginia who witnessed her neighbors suffer and die from the deadly effects of the coal industry.

All four women were moved to fight for specific issues in their respective communities, from brutality to preventable illnesses and a broken healthcare system.

Each was eager to unseat a practically unbeatable male incumbent. Ocasio-Cortez emerged as the only victor. The original and more crucial message in this probing film is that many women might have to fail at least once to succeed.

Lears remarked in many of her interviews that she would run again in the future. With grit and determination, these four women used their fighting spirit to ignore the old rules and take on strong, entrenched opponents. This fight to challenge the status quo is just a beginning.

The candidates highlighted in *Knock Down the House* were genuinely inspired by the hope of changing the US Congress so it would be an accurate representation of the population it serves. They're all working-class women, including two women of color. They had the inspiration and the ability to think quickly on their feet. We can learn almost anything if we are willing to go to the first rung and learn to climb as we go up.

Identifying Unpaid Work and Its Impact

Often, women wonder if they have what it takes to rise to the top. The glass ceiling is commonly referred to as a concrete wall for women of color because of the layers of cultural and social expectations.

In her book *The Moment of Lift*, Melinda Gates talks about unpaid work, which is essentially what family members do to keep a family/household going. This work is unpaid yet essential labor. Gates writes:

> On average, women around the world spend twice as many hours as men on unpaid work, but the range of disparity is wide. In India, women spend six hours a day doing unpaid work, while men spend less than one. In the US, women average more than four hours of unpaid work every day; men average just two-point-five.... There is no country where the gap is zero. This means that, on average, women do seven years more of unpaid work than men over their lifetimes. That's about the time it takes to complete a bachelor's and a master's degree.[19]

Gates discusses unpaid work as a factor in discovering hidden bias and silent inequality.

The impact of unpaid work is huge for women. It not only serves as a barrier toward educational attainment but also toward women in the workforce. Working women are usually still held ac-

19. Gates, Melinda. *The Moment of Lift: How Empowering Women Changes the World*. New York, NY: Flatiron Books, 2019. p. 117.

countable for the majority of unpaid domestic work at home. This trend of having to work a full day in the workforce and then come home and complete the majority of unpaid domestic work is known as the double burden. This burden is the reason many women face multiple challenges to find a balance between their professional and personal lives. The double burden negatively affects women, and even more so, ethnic women who face expectations of strict gender roles. When women spend less time in the workforce than men, males are likely to get promoted over women. The double burden also negatively affects women's wellbeing because it means women have less time for taking care of themselves. This lack of time can also negatively affect their job performance in the workforce, encouraging male promotion over females.

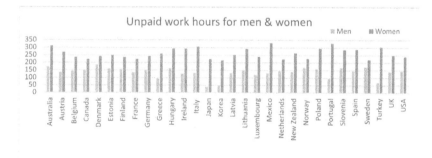

Source: OECD Gender Data Portal based on the OECD Time-Use Database.[20]

Women and men must understand the importance of the fair division of unpaid work. Refer to the unpaid work calculator to track the amount of time you are spending routinely on such duties in your household. Sharing these duties will also promote fair role-playing at home. This silent barrier has limited women in reaching opportunities, and it is time we fight it with a strong voice.

20. OECD. Balancing paid work, unpaid work and leisure. Website. Retrieved from: http://www.oecd.org/gender/balancing-paid-work-unpaid-work-and-leisure.htm

Name:	Preferred Pronoun:		Date:
S. No.	Work	Hour(s)	Minute(s)
1	Laundry		
2	Child Care		
3	Transportation		
4	Meal Preparation		
5	Cleaning		
6	Repairs		
7	Housekeeping		
8	Pet Care		
9	Adult Care		
10	Kids' Schoolwork		
11	Gardening		
12	Shopping		
13	Others		
14			
15			

Why She Must Lead Unpaid Work Calculator www.WhySheMustLead.com

Recharging Through Networking

Women who attempt to climb the leadership ladder often feel so alone within the process. I have been there, and I have felt it. As a woman of color, I initially felt it tricky to put myself out there in venues where other people were different from me in background or appearance. However, with time, I learned that the secret of successful networking lies in choosing the right steps.

The first step is to identify the type of networking group that is best for you. This process could be daunting, especially as a woman of color in a leadership role. But the goal is to surround yourself with amazingly powerful and supportive women. These women can show you the things you can't see yourself. Once you determine which type of networking group is most comfortable for you, start attending that group regularly.

Professional networking is a project of patience and not something you should expect to bear fruit immediately. Let's use the example of building a garden. When you start to build connections, meeting new people is like sowing the seeds. Your goal is that at least some of them will sprout and grow. Therefore, it is essential to keep planting as many of them as possible. Just like a garden, each seed is unique and may not grow right away, but once ready, may bloom the best.

> JUST LIKE GARDENING, BUILDING
> RELATIONSHIPS REQUIRES PATIENCE
> AND TENDING TO YOUR SEEDS.

Once you are in the company of the right network, put in the effort to know everyone in the meeting. The initial meeting isn't about finding who will support you; it is about making links. Use your great personality traits to show that you intend to know the people around you. Your body language can help you, too, by the way you smile and shake hands firmly. You can create influence by making an effort to ask others about their work, their families— anything you can do to help the conversation develop organically and naturally. If someone talks about frustrations or describes some difficult situation, feel free to offer help or advice if you can, but remember, the purpose of these first meetings is to build relationships, not to seal pacts.

Just like gardening, building relationships requires patience and tending to your seeds. You have to keep up with your contacts and offer assistance when they need it. Don't contact them only when you need them. People can be helpful to you in more than one way. Our basic human nature is that we tend to gravitate more toward people whom we befriend. But for a gardener, all the seeds hold the promise of growth. Therefore, even if you are just starting to know someone, they may still become your friend in the future. The purpose of networking is to expand your friends list. Never give up on people without reason. Be patient. Networking is worth your time with the promise of bearing fruit over time as long as you care to grow your garden.

Not Everything Is Important

Choosing your battles often balances on a thin line between knowing what is essential and what to let go. Women are known to worry about performance; therefore, letting go is an outstanding quality to add to your toolkit. When you are in a position where you have the power to fight, use that power when it's necessary. Pick your battles and fight for what matters. This habit will help you stay focused on relevant issues and improve your chances of success in leadership. I suggest asking yourself three questions to determine if the problem is worth the fight:

1. Is this relevant in my day-to-day life?

2. Does it have long-term implications?

3. Will your fight benefit all concerned?

If you answer no to any one of the questions, then reconsider picking that battle. It's important to realize we only have twenty-four hours in a day, and out of that, only a few hours can be productive. It's up to us to choose how we want to use our time. Do we want to spend our day being angry, or do we want to invest our time working toward reaching our goals?

A Closer Look at Criticism

Women can be overcritical about themselves, especially if they are ambitious. It is essential to be open to others' perceptions, especially if they give you honest feedback. Don't get defensive over criticism if it can help you correct or improve your performance. Make room for valid and well-reasoned opinions, both positive and negative. Being open to feedback and accepting it in a friendly way is an essential tool in the leadership kit.

If you adopt a passive, defeated attitude and perceive criticism as personal, your critics may become more aggressive. Therefore, it is crucial to understand that communication skills play a pivotal role in accepting and providing constructive criticism. As a leader, you will be in a situation to evaluate your team's performance and your own. When thinking about communication, remember, face-to-face communication is important when providing feedback to avoid misunderstandings.

Support Other Women Who Are Approaching the First Rung and Beyond

Like Voltaire said, "With great power comes great responsibility." (Uncle Ben in Spiderman comics made this saying famous.) If you are in a leadership position, you have identified at least some of your potential. It is your responsibility as a woman to help other women recognize their potential as well. If you are not advocating, motivating, and encouraging women who work for you, you are part of the problem as well.

IF YOU ARE NOT ADVOCATING, MOTIVATING,
AND ENCOURAGING WOMEN WHO WORK FOR YOU,
YOU ARE PART OF THE PROBLEM AS WELL.

Don't Wait to Be Asked

Most women see leadership as a masculine trait they lack. Women, especially if they are coming from traditional households, wait to be given permission or to be asked before they step up or speak up.

Often, women don't see rising higher in leadership as viable even when they are qualified. It is a similar situation in elected public office. They wait to be asked to run several times before they actually do it.

OFTEN, WOMEN DON'T SEE RISING HIGHER
IN LEADERSHIP AS VIABLE EVEN WHEN THEY ARE
QUALIFIED.

Many women find it hard to speak up for an unpopular opinion and share their thoughts even if they feel strongly about it. They want the topic to come to them before they can express their standing. The essence of leadership lies in balancing the abilities to form fact-based opinions, communicate actively, and navigate challenges. Women are so busy trying to prove themselves that they end up undermining their achievements and selling themselves short. They are thereby waiting to get approval before they can consider stepping up. Eradicating gender bias is made more difficult when women themselves are part of the problem by identifying with specific gender roles and limiting their potential with unconscious bias against their gender.

Unapologetically Own Your Power

Many women shy away from expressing strong opinions or using powerful words. Women in leadership are more often perceived as arrogant compared to their male counterparts. However, being assertive is important, and using the language of power is needed—doing either or both can change people's perception of women as leaders. Women need to avoid talking themselves down, which can prevent them from sharing their knowledge and brilliance with others.

The Only Risk Is Not Trying

Leaders commonly face situations in which they must embrace risk. No matter your profession, your willingness to take risks will set you apart. It can be difficult for many women to embrace uncertainty because they have the added baggage of paradoxes—leaders need to take charge and take risks, but women feel the need to protect their charges, whether children or team. Women must understand that taking a leap of faith is okay; a plan does not have to be perfect to get started because many things can be figured out as you go. What separates women who take risks from others is the drive to step out of their comfort zones and take advantage of opportunities. Risk-taking women know they may fail, but they have faith that they can figure it out as they proceed—whatever it may be. Women need to display courage and believe in their ability to take the bull by horns if they must. Look at the big picture, and ask, "Is it worth it?" If the answer is yes, then move forward.

Meeting women risk-takers was imperative for me in writing this book. One such ambitious woman is my friend Rituja. She originally emigrated from India. She works at Costco, bringing her technological expertise to its systems management process. Rituja is dedicated to issues of equality and justice. She is dedicated to public service beyond her professional role. She serves on the City of Sammamish (Washington State) planning commission, the Sammamish YMCA advisory board, and was appointed to the Washington State Women's Commission by Governor Jay Inslee. She spent more than a decade volunteering as a PTSA board member and has served as treasurer for both the PTSA and the nonprofit, Seattle Globalist.

RISK-TAKING WOMEN KNOW THEY MAY FAIL, BUT THEY HAVE FAITH THAT THEY CAN FIGURE IT OUT AS THEY PROCEED—WHATEVER IT MAY BE.

Last year, Rituja ran for the city council for the second time. It was heartbreaking for me to see such a formidable leader and friend lose twice. She explained the uphill battle she confronted when she chose to run. "The city council in Sammamish doesn't sound or look like me," she said. "When I looked around, I did not see people like me being mentored or encouraged to run for office. I decided to step up and say, 'I am ready.'"

Rituja explained her loss in the election as the pushback that women of color are bound to get when they step up. "We don't have to just settle for the image of who we think a politician is supposed to be. And I am not giving up just because of a lost race." To this day, she continues to challenge the status quo. Racial justice is not an auxiliary issue because it directly affects women of color. As more women of color become leaders, they continue to move toward center stage, with growing calls to focus on the systemic issues that plague the communities they belong to.

Rituja explained, "We have to be systematic in our efforts to break the norms. We have to change the way we perceive politics in our communities." When asked if she is ready to take the bull by horns, she laughs, "You are right! I have always chosen to fight for equity."

Rituja spoke about the sense of powerlessness constituents sometimes feel. "People have seen their communities remain the same regardless of who is in elected offices," she said. "It is crucial that we as residents and taxpayers (and not only when we become citizens) know that our voice matters, that we participate in civic engagement and create grassroots movements that address issues in our communities. We need to organize, educate, and not shy away from politics."

"I'm an immigrant and a woman of color," Rituja proclaimed. "I am aware of my race, my gender, my socio-economic standing, and my privilege. All these inform and empower me to continue to fight for injustice and to create an equal world each day," she continued.

Recent studies project people of color will be the majority in the United States by 2045, with women of color primed to be the majority of women by 2060.[21] Women are already the country's largest growing voting community, and women of color are the fastest-growing segment of that group. This fact hints at the future of the political landscape and how women of color are destined to shape it, be it as a voter or a leader. We all must embrace the facts and learn

---

21. Older People Projected to Outnumber Children for First Time in US History. https://www.census.gov/newsroom/press-releases/2018/cb18-41-population-projections.html.

from risk-takers and their successes and failures so that the country can shift to principled leadership.

Key in the Key People

You may have the ambition; you may have the skill, but if decision-makers aren't aware of what you are aiming for, it's possible to miss out on great opportunities. Communication is the key. You can never overcommunicate when it comes to keeping your intentions about the next big role you want to take on be made clear and known.

TAKEAWAYS

A higher number of women are entering the workforce than ever before. But the disparity at the top is still huge. Women must challenge the status quo and push the limits with resilience. Women need to conduct their research to identify what they can build on and where their strengths lie. Test the crucial behaviors I have identified so far, and don't be afraid to apply what you've learned and experiment.

Whether you learn best practices for igniting your career on your own or from others, the point remains the same: Find what works for you and let that dictate your path. You can contribute to making workplaces work for women if you can build belief in the importance of change and implement it in the workplace.

Don't be afraid to tell your story—the whole story—to show the struggles are worth it, and you can succeed.

SELF-REFLECTION EXERCISE:
REACHING YOUR SKY

1. Describe a perfect day at your workplace and include all things you want to happen.

    _____
    _____
    _____

2. What practices and policies of your workplace are helping you to achieve your dream?

    _____
    _____
    _____

3. Is there anything missing in your workplace culture, which is impacting your belonging? Or is there a way to improve your belonging?

    _____
    _____
    _____

4. Have you identified an effective way to communicate the missing ideas that can help in workplace culture?

    _____
    _____
    _____

5. Pledge to create or find new avenues to network, which align with your vision of growth.

    _____
    _____
    _____

CHAPTER 4

RISING ABOVE BARRIERS: INCLUSION MATTERS

*"Every woman's success should be an inspiration to another.
We're strongest when we cheer each other on."*

— **Serena Williams**

I often wonder: Is it enough to have an agenda of inclusion to advance women?

Before we dive into this question, I want to discuss my examples of when I got promoted to a leadership role. My challenge was still not over with advancement. Let's see what happened in my situation.

I switched to a management role within a few years of my career. I learned through experience that in the healthcare industry, the problem is not about inducting women. More women than men work in healthcare. The main issue is the failure to promote women to leadership roles. Although women make up the majority of healthcare workers in the US, a tiny percentage of healthcare CEOs are women. The healthcare industry, unlike other industries, does not have a "women in healthcare" problem but a "women not leading in healthcare" problem.

It's surprising to know that leadership positions in healthcare are significantly skewed toward men, despite women making up 70 percent of the healthcare workforce. The imbalance is more pronounced in the case of women of color. Women, overall, make up approximately 30 percent of C-suite teams and only 5 percent of leadership positions.[22]

Let's dissect my story. When I was promoted to Director of Rehab in 2013, I had an infant at home. It was a daunting task to balance both child and career, so I worked on identifying and minimizing my barriers. I call these barriers the Three Ms: 1) Motherhood—I was able to survive growing childcare costs and find reliable support for my kids, 2) Mentorship—I requested a mentor to get the guidance, and I was told I would have one, and 3) Money, or pay gap—I negotiated well to receive my fair share.

Nevertheless, even with increased awareness of these concepts, I stepped down from my role within five years and decided to continue as a clinician. I know you must be wondering why I did so.

The reason I passed on the position was it did not feel right. I felt like a misfit. Not much made me feel like I belonged. So, I was trying to outperform so much that I went to work seven days a week, despite being salaried, which meant being paid for fixed hours only. Ultimately, my leadership position was unreasonably stressful.

I felt like an alien because I was the only brown woman in the leadership group, and there was a general lack of connection or visibility.

I grew up in a culture where women spoke minimally. They were discouraged from lengthy discussions or decision-making; a subset of elders in the family usually made important decisions. This barrier made me sell myself short, and I did not broadcast or highlight my accomplishments.

---

22. World Economic Forum. "7 out of 10 global health leaders are men." Website. Retrieved from: https://www.weforum.org/agenda/2020/04/global-health-leadership-gender-equality-report/.

I have always had an urge to advance my skills, but when I wanted to further my education while in a leadership role, I was told I was on my own due to budget cuts. Education benefits in the workplace had shrunk in recent years, and I had to relinquish my role because no opportunities existed to advance my skills.

I had to continually guard against judgments about being a new mom and holding a leadership position. I made time to socialize with coworkers, even if it took away from personal time with family. This behavior made me overcompensate in social situations, causing a stressful work-life imbalance. However, I did not find the support that would have empowered me to gain better insight into the position and culture and help me continue as a leader.

Even though I requested a mentor, it was still challenging for me to find a mentor who could guide me in a leadership role. I was good at my job and achieved my goals, but having a mentor would have helped me and my peers overcome bias and promote an inclusive environment.

The above issues were not due to a lack of inclusionary practices, but rather, the problem was in the way inclusion was handled—which wasn't helpful in my case.

To dig further into my quest for inclusion, I got together with Amy Bhatt over coffee. Amy is a prolific writer about community formation and activism for South Asian immigrants. She is an associate professor of gender and women's studies and an affiliate associate professor in the language, literacy, and culture program and the Asian studies program at the University of Maryland, Baltimore County (UMBC). She completed her PhD in feminist studies from the University of Washington in Seattle, Washington. I find her to be an excellent resource for exploring more deeply into immigrant women's experiences in the workplace.

Amy's passion and dedication to women's empowerment inspired me a great deal. I was taken by her during our meeting as she shared snippets from her most recent book *High-Tech Housewives: Indian IT Workers, Gendered Labor, and Transmigration*. Her writing highlights Indian migrants in IT and the struggles they face with family obligations, career paths, citizenship, and a sense of belonging as they move between South Asia and the United States. Immigrant women often face microaggression (explained more in the next section of this chapter) at work because they lack representation in leadership. Companies can't add female representation overnight. However, they can use several strategies to improve immigrant women's experiences.

Companies can first pay thorough attention to teams or functions where women are hardly visible. Moreover, they should be deliberate about staffing. Staffing should be very conscious of diversity. Companies can improve diverse females' experiences by helping women build links with each other through mentorship programs or by recruiting them for cross-functional projects.

Interviewing Amy helped me understand the needed behavior shift if workplaces are to be inclusive of women like us. I then conducted further interviews to diagnose the barriers to inclusion.

WHAT IS EXCLUDING US?

Microaggressions

Columbia University professor Derald Sue used the term "microaggression" to refer to intentional or unintentional daily workplace humiliation that gives rise to aggressive or negative racial insults toward people of color. This term was coined by renowned psychiatrist Dr. Chester Pierce in the 1970s.

The concept of microaggression has been around for a long time, and we are still trying to overcome it. Many women report that they still experience gender-based microaggression in the workplace.

If managers condemn gender-biased language and attitudes, women in the workplace will feel significantly happier and more confident. And they are likely to stay longer. However, there are few such managers.

MICROAGGRESSION:
INTENTIONAL OR UNINTENTIONAL DAILY
WORKPLACE HUMILIATION THAT GIVES RISE
TO AGGRESSIVE OR NEGATIVE RACIAL
INSULTS TOWARD PEOPLE OF COLOR.

Almost 64 percent of women face microaggression in the workplace. Consequently, women have to prove their capabilities more than men do.

These statistics make sense when we understand what microaggression is. However, the question is, what does microaggression look like in action?

After considerable research and several interviews, I find microaggression often falls into one of two camps: 1) biased actions that feel prejudiced, or 2) comments indicating, at best, insensitivity and, at worst, derogatory views.

When people hear the word microaggression, they generally associate it with little things that hurt people's feelings. However, from a broader perspective, it isn't just about hurt feelings. It's about how being repeatedly abandoned, humiliated, and invalidated intensifies the disparity in power and privilege and leads to racism and discrimination.

Some examples listed by a variety of women I interviewed are:

1. "You speak good English"—This comment seems like a compliment, doesn't it? It is not. Its underlying meaning is offensive because it identifies a person as a foreigner in the workplace. It leads to isolation.

2. "What she's trying to say is...."—Have you ever faced a situation where a colleague, primarily male, interrupted or talked over you in a meeting? If you are a woman, I am sure you must have been through it at some point. This interruption is referred to as "mansplaining." Merriam-Webster defines mansplaining as the moment when "a man talks condescendingly to someone (especially a woman) about something he has incomplete knowledge of, with the mistaken assumption that he knows more about it than the person he's talking to does."[23]

3. "Where did you go to high school? Do you understand how it is done here?"—Women are often asked to provide more proof of qualifications than necessary.

4. "I don't see race. There is only one race, the human race."—This is denying the individual as a racial/cultural being.

5. "Why are you so quiet? Be more verbal. Speak up more." Some women report facing situations where they were uncomfortable speaking up due to observed microaggressive behaviors in their environment. Instead of getting the source of the problem eliminated, they were asked to speak up more, leading to ineffective communication.

---

23. Merriam-Webster. (n.d.). Mansplaining. In Merriam-Webster.com dictionary. Retrieved July 8, 2020, from https://www.merriam-webster.com/words-at-play/mansplaining-definition-history.

"I think we have covered everyone." This statement looks harmless, but it can be an issue if, due to lack of visibility, women were not given a chance to speak or ask questions in a meeting. Some women have reported that their presence was ignored because they looked or sounded different from the rest of the team leading to more barriers.

What Can Be Done?

Microaggressions negatively impact the culture of inclusion. The best solution is to understand what behaviors and actions constitute microaggressions and how harmful it can be to the workplace environment. Managers and decision-makers have a central role in filtering out microaggression by training, education, and reinforcement. But complete prevention is probably impossible until any form of discrimination and lack of awareness exists. So how should anyone respond to the microaggressions they face in the workplace?

Subtle comments are hard to call out and can be emotionally draining to confront. Reacting immediately may label you as overly sensitive or make the person you call out defensive. It is best to keep your calm and use a thoughtful approach. I call it an AAA framework to decide a course of action:

- **Analyze:** Do not feel compelled to respond to every case; give yourself power to decide what needs your attention. Let yourself experience the emotion that comes to you—disappointment, anger, frustration, or anything else. But don't act on impulse. Use your discretion to understand what happened and who did it. Analyze how important the issue or person is to you. Is it worth your comment or silence?

- **Address:** If your analysis warrants an action, then prepare yourself to address it appropriately. This needs to be a tactful conversation. You have to set the ground fairly by giving them opportunity to realize why it is important to be discussed and what can be done to avoid future incidences. Let them unpack what happened and explain their intent. Acknowledge and accept what they are trying to mean. But reinforce that intent doesn't replace impact. Appreciate their time to clarify their intent and express hope they appreciate your willingness to clarify their impact.

- **Allow:** Allow the impact appropriately. Don't let microaggression overpower you in anyway. You need to control what affects you. There is a greater empowerment in protecting your peace and happiness.

Access to Resources

We have talked about gender discrimination. However, bias doesn't exist between men and women only. Discrimination against women from different cultures and ethnicities is also prevalent.

WOMEN OF COLOR HAVE LESS ACCESS TO
SENIOR LEADERS THAN WHITE WOMEN.

Women of color get even less support from their managers than other minority groups. Women of color have less access to senior leaders than white women. This disparity is quite unfavorable for them because employees who are regularly in touch with senior leaders have more chances of getting promoted, becoming leaders, and staying at their companies. The situation is critical for black women. They have far fewer resources when it comes to organizational politics and maintaining work-life balance. Moreover, managers don't give them due credit for their accomplishments.

The same dynamic holds for access to managers. Very few black women meet their manager outside of work, compared to white women to build professional relationship. Similarly, women at the entry-level are less likely to have managers praise their work and help them navigate organizational politics than men at the same level. Compared to white women, women of color have little opportunity to interact with senior leaders, formally or informally. Black women have the least access to senior leaders.

What Can Be Done?

Leaders in any organization can help the women of color on their teams to advance. There has to be a bridge in gaps created by the bias. I discuss below an easy "Check and Connect" strategy to create equal access to leadership.

- *Check for hidden bias.* There has been an increased awareness to check for discrimination in reviews and promotions by gender in recent years, but unless outcomes are studied in regards to race and gender, it will not much solve the problem. The comparison of hiring and advancement rate between peers and women of color is essential to track to ensure the success of inclusion efforts.

- *Check that visibility is even.* This can be achieved by giving credit for good work where due and fair. It does not mean singing praises more for minority employees but making sure they are not ignored due to any reason that can exclude them. A positive working environment will create great connections. Even while providing feedback, make sure you do not become defensive or overprotective. Demonstrating that you care deeply about advancement and opportunities everyone gets will go a long way in creating trust in women of color.

- *Check if you invite them.* This is needed to overcome the loss of missed opportunities for socialization. Include your intent in the invitation by stating that you look forward to getting to know them better. If there is appropriate personal outreach with clear communication, it will be perceived as an honest attempt to include everyone in professional meetups.

- *Check if you factor in potential* and not just performance. When only a few women of color have leadership roles, it can be inadvertent for managers to consider just a few observed performances as an example to predict how they will grow. This view can have the unintended consequence of excluding women of color. It's equally important to look for determination and a sense of purpose, which are also indicators for future leadership potential.

- *Check if you have asked why they are quitting.* Not every company has a mandatory exit interview policy for employees that systematically checks who is leaving and why. These conversations are crucial because they can provide much-needed insight into the experiences of women of color. It is an opportunity for workplaces and organizations to fix their leaky talent pipeline.

Women of color hold great potential as future leaders. In modern times, when workplaces are emerging as more diverse, women of color mustn't be left behind.

Imbalance in Hiring and Promotions

Do you know what the two most significant factors for changing the representation of women in entry-level positions are? Hiring and promotion. Unfortunately, companies don't hire and promote women and men at equal rates. Most of the time, if reviewers are not trained on how to eliminate unconscious bias, then it can aggravate the situation. These untrained reviewers don't give equal consideration to women, people of color, and other underrepresented groups. As a result, some companies lag in recruiting diverse candidates, and even fewer are consider them for promotions.

What Can Be Done?

There is a need that almost every company must provide unconscious bias training to employees involved in hiring. The training must be a requirement for employees engaged in performance reviews. The companies and the organizations supporting the enterprises must encourage employees to take steps to avoid bias at the outset of both processes.

The irony is that very few companies have end-to-end processes in place to ensure fair practices. Unconscious bias often dictates who gets hired. We can't expect to see any progress for women in the workplace until companies begin to hire and promote women at the same rate as men.

When managers are firmly against discrimination, employees are more likely to think everyone has an equal chance to progress at work regardless of their gender.

The inclusive behavior of a manager is particularly important to women. When managers oppose gender biases, women are less likely to think their gender is holding them back and more likely to believe they enjoy the same opportunities as their peers.

Men think leaders are doing a better job of promoting gender diversity than women think they do. Men must access how much managers challenge gender-biased language and behavior. Men must also be advocates and ensure senior leaders offer guidance on how to advance women and improve gender diversity.

FEWER WOMEN THINK LEADERS ARE CHALLENGING GENDER BIAS.

Emotional Tax Burden

In the healthcare field, I have worked with employees with diverse backgrounds: Asian, Black, Latino, and multiracial. They all aspire to advance and contribute to their organizations. Most of them have agreed with me in different ways about their constant state of being "on guard." It is a protective mechanism against potential bias because of their gender or cultural background. I wonder if, eventually, this constant battle negatively affects their health, wellbeing, and ability to prosper at work.

It was true in my case. As a woman of color, I felt "on guard" too. As a result, I focused on outworking and outperforming my colleagues to prove myself. This pressure leads to stress and burnout. As a result, I often developed a desire to leave my work for both my mental and physical wellbeing. Interestingly, despite these challenges, I always had a desire to contribute and progress. I constantly looked for challenging and intellectually stimulating work and wanted to apply for higher positions.

What Can Be Done?

I believe that employers can play an active role in losing their talent pool by minimizing the consequences of this emotional burnout.

The missing action is the *innovative* practices of inclusion. Inclusion is an intentional process that requires considerable insight and planning on the part of the employer. But in today's world, it's an indispensable step for companies trying to retain their most talented, qualified, and motivated workers. The best part is that a culture of inclusion does not require a significant investment. It mainly involves awareness and advocacy. And, most important is the *intention*.

The big takeaway from my experience is that women don't need to be told to pursue leadership. Research shows that most of them are confident, ambitious, and determined when it comes to their profession.

The question is: When women of color share the same workplace as the rest of the population, why do they face such vastly different experiences in advancement?

Women of color in the United States held only 4 percent of C-suite offices in 2018, falling far below white men, at 68 percent and white women at 19 percent.[24] Why are they so outnumbered? In my experience, I have seen workplaces have tried. There has been a significant push to include women in top roles by hiring and promoting women in all leadership positions and offering them C-suite offices. I feel there is a need to research and evaluate employee experiences from the perspective of women of color. A closer look is needed, especially in the key areas that influence their desire to stay with their companies.

By 2060, the census projects that women of color could be in the majority. However, without intervention, the already-low percentage of women of color at the management and executive levels may drop further. Women of color could hold fair representation

---

24. Washington, Z. (2019). "Women of Color Get Less Support at Work. Here's How Managers Can Change That." *Harvard Business Review*. Retrieved from: https://hbr.org/2019/03/women-of-color-get-less-support-at-work-heres-how-managers-can-change-that.

in top positions by the next decade if companies adopt effective and non-discriminatory strategies for hiring and promotion. It is essential to understand that for the diversity and inclusion plan to be complete, every woman needs to feel she has a fair chance to pursue her dream. The focus needs to be on hiring and *retaining* women of color. Efforts need to be made to reach out to non-profit, entrepreneurial, or entertainment industries as well.

OF ALL THE BARRIERS FOR WORKING WOMEN, UNEVEN SUPPORT IS THE MOST DAMAGING AND ENDURING.

An equal opportunity moves people together toward empowerment, but unequal support does the reverse. Of all the barriers for working women, uneven support is the most damaging and enduring. Without an explicit effort to achieve that equity in support, workplaces will never be completely inclusive. The status quo will result in even less inclusion. Yet, most workplaces are working to be more inclusive and minimize the disparity between the numbers of men and women in leadership. But the goal, of course, is not just to ensure women are seen in equal numbers in the workforce; the goal is to remove the barriers that keep them from taking on leadership roles. And those barriers are more significant for women of color than any other group.

All the workplaces I've visited and all the data I have seen have convinced me that race and gender have a significant impact on workplace experience. Employers cannot just go with a one-size-fits-all-women approach and ignore the unique cultural backgrounds and opinions of women of color. Organizations that do not pay attention to issues like these lose the opportunity to benefit from diversity. Women of color must continuously fight biases against their gender, race, ethnicity, and sometimes religion.

I'm reminded of an example from early in my career. We had an employee of color who did not eat meat due to her cultural preferences. Everyone at work was aware of her preference because she made sure we did not accidentally offer her food she wouldn't eat. She always brought her lunch, even when there were work lunch events where takeout food was ordered. The manager wanted her to be included in the takeout meals—we were all asked not to bring food because the manager would provide lunch. One of the office manager's tasks was to order the food for everyone, so she ended up ordering pizza to keep it simple but did not factor in giving an option in food choice. When lunch arrived, there was only pepperoni pizza. It was okay for everyone except this one coworker. She inquired if there was any other choice available. Although she was invited to join the meal, the only suggestion they had was for her to try removing the pepperoni topping and eating the rest of the pizza. She looked a little perplexed and decided to skip lunch that day.

That was one of the examples for me of a failed attempt to connect in the workplace. Although the food preference situation is not exclusive for women of color, cultural backgrounds do play a role in their experiences with others in their working environment. I could see she grew uncomfortable with being authentic at work after this incident and began to hide other aspects of her life because she felt a lack of understanding or sensitivity toward her cultural and religious needs. This is the very thing that can make work-life balance even harder for women of color than it is for the majority of women.

Women of Color Want to Stay

Indeed, job satisfaction, career paths, and workplace culture are not aligned with what women of color expect. I have discussed how a feeling of belonging that corresponds with a woman's abilities to maintain long-term careers is the key to their retention in a company. Their experience can be enhanced with leadership roles. In the workplace, when women of color feel equal to everyone, they are more assertive and able to defend their goals. Workplaces with better retention of female leaders of color help see that when women are not always on guard with their peers and superiors due to their cultural or ethnic identities, they can focus better on their jobs and improve relationships with peers.

The lack of a sense of belonging can worsen the leadership gap for women of color. An understanding of how belonging and leadership are linked holds the key to resolving the issue. I have seen how cohesiveness gels diversity. I have also seen it as an example for myself. That is why I am passionate about employers who support women of color, not just with promotions, but also by helping them stay and grow.

When the environment around women offers understanding and trust, they can start to break their barriers as they engage in opportunities fully and add to their skills. As they grow as leaders, they can see their talent. As they develop their abilities, they can see their capabilities and can speak up for equality, not only for themselves but for their cohorts as well. That is what happens when employers offer the right environment for women of color. The women rise and grow.

TAKEAWAYS

A little knowledge is harmful, especially when it comes to an understanding of women of color's experiences in workplaces. There is much talk about inclusion as diversity becomes widespread, but action lags. One common reason for this lag is the lack of information or feedback needed to understand and apply effective inclusion strategies in the workplace. It is equally important that people who value inclusion have adequate information to judge the success of such procedures correctly. Lack of knowledge can easily lead to tokenism, which is worse than negligence. Therefore, there is a considerable need for research when it comes to creating a fact-based strategy about inclusion in the workplace. Lots of reports over the years have classified women in a generic sense. These studies fail to address the experience of women of color and the barriers they face, thereby leaving out big pieces of the puzzle when it comes to inequality. Employers need to take moral responsibility for zooming in on and observing behaviors, actions, and policies that keep minority women underrepresented in the workforce and in management. Similarly, every woman owes it to every other woman to stand up for the next one in line. Whatever category of women we belong to, we need to flex our resilience muscle and work at building connections for fighting inequality.

SELF-REFLECTION EXERCISE:
RISING ABOVE BARRIERS: INCLUSION MATTERS

1. Identify examples of inclusive behavior.

    _____

    _____

    _____

    _____

2. What are your personality traits that can help your communication in a diverse group?

    _____

    _____

    _____

    _____

3. Have you ever experienced or witnessed microaggression in your workplace?

    _____

    _____

    _____

4. List a few examples of discriminatory behavior that can happen in the workplace.

    _____

    _____

    _____

5. What steps will you take to address discriminatory behaviors when observed?

    _____

    _____

    _____

CHAPTER 5

SURPASSING YOUR LIMITS

RECRUIT, ATTEND, CARE, EVOLVE

"We need women at all levels, including the top, to change the dynamic, reshape the conversation, to make sure women's voices are heard and heeded, not overlooked, and ignored."

— **Sheryl Sandberg**

About a year ago, when I started to write this book, I had just heard about the State of Womxn of Color Summit in Seattle. And no, I have not misspelled the word "women" like most of you must be thinking. The founders of this summit deliberately included the X in women. I will come back to that at the end of the chapter. For now, let's talk about the origin of this summit before diving into the details.

The State of Womxn of Color Summit

This summit was the brainchild of a Seattle-based career platform, "Future for Us." What makes this platform extraordinary is its dedication to advancing women of color in various areas. The platform came to life when co-founder Sage Ke'alohilani Quiamno realized a huge gap existed in the market when it came to work and community-building opportunities for women of color. The founders spoke at more than 100 events in 2018 to express how women of color had very little visibility at decision-making tables. Women of color were either forgotten or pushed aside whenever it came to talking about women's empowerment. Not many women of color were given the voice needed to speak out on issues in the community. The public did not notice how prevalent the problem of pushing women of color aside was until the Future For Us decided to take their message a step further by creating a summit for women of different ethnicities. The summit's goal was to help the public understand why it was essential to include all types of women, regardless of their race, religion, and sexuality.

Sage recreates seats of power for and by womxn of color so that our workforce reflects what womxn of color bring to the table: resilience, ROI (return on investment), and liberation. She is a Hawaiian and an activist for issues related to women of color. She has excellent recognition as an entrepreneur. She is credited as a co-founder of Future For Us, a platform dedicated to advancing womxn of color through community, culture, and career development. Sage has galvanized a nationwide movement to build a future of work that reaches new growth levels through diversity, equity, and inclusion.

Her initial career includes work on pay equity. She provided over four thousand women with the tools and resources they needed to advocate for themselves. Her efforts were remarkable in results; women were able to negotiate $500K in salary increases and secure 150 promotions. Sage is an amplifier, promoting for womxn of color at work in top publications and organizations—from Forbes,

Fast Company, Entrepreneur, and Geekwire to SXSW, the Women's March, Microsoft, Starbucks, and more.

Sage has gathered an outpouring amount of recognition and support. Her accolades indicate that our communities and workplaces are ready to fight for equity. She has been honored recently with Rising Star Awards from Seattle's National Organization for Women and the Seattle Metropolitan Chamber of Commerce. She has been granted the University of Washington's Community Leadership Award and a nomination for Forbes 30 Under 30 Class of 2020. In the year 2019, she was recognized as one of Seattle's Most Influential People of 2019 by *Seattle Magazine*.

The summit was a series of events that incorporated statistical data, storytelling, and strategies for women of color and their allies. The purpose of these events was to create a place for women where they could be seen, valued, and supported as they thrived regardless of the race they belonged to.

After reading about this summit and researching the Future for Us, I was inspired because I saw I was not the only one striving to bring change for women of color. The launch of this great startup was a revolutionary moment for all women all over the world. More than 300 people were in a room with one of the most diverse groups Seattle had ever seen. The launch was their first step in eradicating the stereotypes many people hold about people of color. Unfortunately, people just do not realize how harmful stereotypes can be.

When You Meet a Strong Woman, You Feel the Strength Inside You

My vision is quite simple—women of color deserve to lead at the highest levels across all sectors. Therefore, it was imminent for me to connect with this organization as it has worked tirelessly to light the path for women of color working to lead at the highest levels in all sectors. Its members have worked diligently on building community and uplifting the culture of women of color. One top priority for me was getting an interview with Sage Ke'alohilani Quiamno. She was excited to hear about my book and gladly invited me to meet with her.

During the interview, I asked her what inspired her to come up with this revolutionary idea. She told me that the McKinsey's 2018 Women in the Workplace report fired her and other women of color up and set them on this journey. According to that report, women of color struggled much harder to gain leadership roles in their companies compared to men. Women of color are intelligent, inspiring, and ready to lead, but they are not provided the same opportunities white women are offered. The potential of women of color is undeniable, but we are often made to believe otherwise. Women of color are the fastest-growing segment of the population, and yet they have the least say when it comes to topics such as the wage gap. A large percentage of women of color hold degrees and are new hires, but only a handful are C-suite executives.

Sage is determined to increase this percentage so more women of color will be in better positions to stand up for equity. She informed me why it was essential to break these barriers before everyone behind it could crumble. It fascinated me that Womxn of Color is working to help other women progress. Her main objective is to see other women of color prosper in their professional lives.

I was also quite intrigued by why the word "women" is spelled "womxn," so I asked her about it.

"The spelling of womxn is meant to show inclusion of transgender, non-binary, womxn of color, womxn with disabilities, and all other marginalized genders. Future for Us uses this spelling to indicate that our platform is open to anyone who identifies as such. We respect people of all genders, identities, and the use of pronouns that best identify an individual," Sage explained.

Isn't it amazing how Womxn of Color is not only including women of color, but also women from different sexualities and all marginalized women? There was more than just one objective behind this movement, and that has made this foundation successful.

After talking with this powerhouse woman of color, I was amazed that her stories exactly mirrored mine. We need networks like these for *every* woman who may face discrimination. I cannot help but anticipate the changes that will take place if we can create such a drive and leadership for marginalized women in every nook of the world. If Sage can achieve so much in a year, imagine what magic women can do standing up for each other in the rest of the world.

I look forward to celebrating that moment, and I hope support for women of color in leadership reaches across the country like a fire. We have proven examples that all it takes to bring change around the country is determination and strength.

When you ignite connection, collaboration, and a sense of community among women who were underprivileged for any reason, you grow with the cause. Women will realize they are not alone in their struggles—that it is a nationwide problem. We are not asking for our rights, but rather, we are demanding them. It is even more challenging to fight for simple rights if you are a woman of color. I am not saying this to create a divide among women fighting for their rights. It is to remind all that discrimination also exists within our gender. The ceiling is multi-layered. Those layers include culture, religion, background, patriarchal influences, and ideologies in their society. This message is what we want to convey as we all stand together for the same rights.

This book's main objective is to create a future where we are aware and organized to fight discrimination among women themselves when it comes to color, race, ethnicity, and disabilities. We need to build a strong community so our problems can be discussed in a common dialogue in every pocket of the world. The only way we can create solutions is by talking about the problems and dissecting them. Conversations can set the stage for solutions. There will always be a certain group of people who will not accept that their system has failed us. But my goal through this book is to pave a path for women of color to present the issues they face even while living in a First-World country.

Challenges Follow Women Everywhere— Proportions Increase with Minorities

Many may think women in the US have fewer barriers, but we face a different set of problems daily. The ceiling remains concrete for women of color. We have made spectacular advances professionally, especially as entrepreneurs, but not many people are aware of these advancements. And let me tell you one interesting fact: Latina-owned businesses are the fastest-growing segment of the women-owned business market. These businesses are starting up at six times the national average according to statistics. But there's a catch in the situation that will make you take a step back and realize how womxn of color are placed at a disadvantage.

According to Sage, the disparity in income is a significant barrier when it comes to equity for women of color:

> There may be an increase in women-led business ventures, yet our earnings and net wealth are pale compared to that of white women and men. Due to inequitable access to opportunities, by the end of our careers, our white peers have over $1 million

more in wealth. Now imagine everything that's possible with a million dollars! As per PayScale's Compensation Best Practices Report, about 66 percent of employers don't intend to analyze race or gender pay equity. So, the use of this statistic can be a great plan to advocate for women of color so they can be promoted to different leadership roles.

But workplaces and statistics are only one part of the equation. What can we do as a cohort of women to make what we do count? Every successful reform has found support inside the organization. Women need inside allies. We know this, so where disparity exists in pay or opportunities, women must raise questions, even if it leads to difficult conversations.

How can we use this awareness and activism in day-to-day life? During the interview, Sage identified these golden rules:

- Acknowledge the women who came to the picture before you.

- Ensure equitable access to resources across your team.

- Create thriving policies for everyone.

- Acknowledge your opportunities, bias, and blind spots.

- Be an active ally for women of color, no matter who you are.

When workplaces lack equity, diversity, and inclusion, they are less productive, and the talent pool is shallow. Most of the energy is diverted from lifting people up to keeping people down. Women's access to the workforce may have improved, but around the world, women get paid less than men; minority women, or women of color, get paid even less. They also have even less opportunity for advancement or promotion. Unless women get equal opportunities, workplaces will continue to struggle with employee retention. Stable and diverse workplaces are the cradles that nurture equity in the modern world.

GOT "RACE"?

The layers of gender and race make the wage gap a complicated situation. A considerable gap exists when it comes to providing opportunities, from recruitment and retention to promotions. If we are going to highlight the racial gender pay gap, we must talk about the opportunity gap as well. Why do some women have more opportunities than others based on race?

When I started writing this book, I studied a lot of research about the inequities women of color face in the workplace. Most of the data focused on the pay gap between men and women. However, I always felt that before the pay gap, the issue that needs consideration is the opportunity gap and removing unconscious bias. We can solve a problem only when we know what the root cause is. First, we need to come up with a solution to break down entry barriers for women of color. After a lot of research, interviews, and brainstorming, I came up with four major factors responsible for the opportunity gap. I call them RACE.

RACE stands for Recruit, Attend, Care, and Evolve. It consists of four tactics to help executives and individuals strengthen inclusivity for women of color. Let's look at each tactic in detail.

1. Recruit

Recruiting women of color is a crucial step toward welcoming diversity. There is a need to make the recruiting process free of any unconscious biases. There has been a lot of discussion about improving diversity by blind hiring. Although the concept of blind hiring isn't new, the strategy of hiding certain candidate information until the late stages of the recruiting process has become more prevalent in recent years, thanks to advancements in technology. It may not be the right solution for every organization. It also needs to be evaluated whether the practice prevents discrimination in the long run. But it's still worth a shot in shifting demographics and expanding the talent pool where possible.

So, what about workplaces that lack the resources to implement a sophisticated blind recruiting program?

What will be important is to use some creativity and thoughtfulness to create a sense of diverse culture that aligns with the charter. It can be the main decisive factor for diverse women when deciding to apply for a job. Therefore, work on the retention of women of color in leadership roles begins with recruitment. If they feel welcomed, chances are they will stay with the organization for an extended period. During the interview phase, the interviewer needs to be friendly and open to listening. This behavior is beneficial for the company because, when women of color are interviewed, they will not fathom isolation even if they may be a minority in office. They also see healthy work relationships and the environment. Women of color like to stay associated with organizations where they get visibility and acknowledgment, just like the rest of the employees.

Women of color, particularly those formerly incarcerated, have trouble finding suitable jobs after serving their sentences. Already riddled with problems such as racism and sexism, these women often end up settling for part-time jobs, which barely allow them to pay their bills. The following survey, conducted by prisonpolicy.org,[25] demonstrates the clear difference between formerly incarcerated women of color and men while trying to get a full-time job. While the difference might not be significant, it is far from equal.

---

25. Couloute, Kopf (2018). Out or Prison & Out of Work. Retrieved from: https://www.prisonpolicy.org/reports/outofwork.html; Bureau of Justice https://www.bjs.gov/content/pub/pdf/p16.pdf.

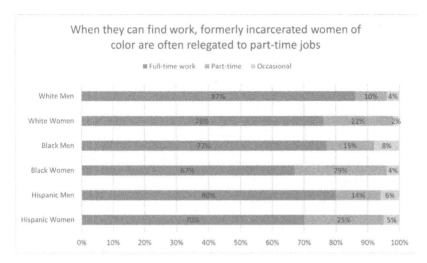

Source: U.S. Bureau of Justice Statistics National Former Prison Survey

2. Attend

Women who are promoted may spend their days doing diligent work, but without a sense of belonging, they may never achieve their goals. This reality applies to millions of women of color who work in environments that don't prioritize inclusivity and its benefits. More companies are beginning to navigate the complexities of fostering diversity in the workplace. Many recent social movements have driven Fortune 500 companies to appoint chief diversity officers (CDO) to view diversity as a business issue. However, a CDO is not enough to ensure diversity initiatives succeed. Such executives can only help in an environment where the resources needed to make their initiatives a reality are in place.

Employers who "walk the talk" can have better retention. It is important to strive to minimize favoritism to build an equal pitch for all employees. Employers need to hold every leader accountable for the results of efforts promoting diversity and inclusion. There must be an environment of constant coaching to ensure inclusion efforts are effective. To drive the change, employers need to keep their senses open so they can see and hear the perceptions and experiences of women of color. Employers should have a plan for active problem-solving catering to the individual structure and employee groups in their workplace.

3. Care

Caring is the most powerful and most underused force for creating positive change in the world. You don't hear about care in business discussions or debates, but it is the basis of most social justice movements around the world. For me, care is the effort that helps others flourish and is often the simplest thing to do, and it is free.

> CARING IS THE MOST POWERFUL AND MOST UNDERUSED FORCE FOR CREATING A POSITIVE CHANGE IN THE WORLD.

You don't need to be an employee's friend to give them care. Care can be given without commitments, negotiations, and compromises. Use mini-positive interactions with *everyone* included in your day-to-day operations and as the basis of individual relationships where all employees feel safe to express and display emotions. Work environments must have spheres of care so that people can receive support and withstand stress. Care can transform how women experience work because they feel like part of a group and feel valued. Care also involves employers speaking up and being advocates for equality. Constant evaluation of work culture is essential and should lead to changes in practices not contributing to equity.

CARE CAN BE GIVEN WITHOUT COMMITMENTS, NEGO-
TIATIONS, AND COMPROMISES.

4. Evolve

Women of color have often reported less satisfaction than white women with their ability to achieve long-term career goals. If a woman is not satisfied with the available opportunities to improve job-related skills, she is likely to leave the organization. This isolation is the result of a lack of connection, visibility, and support. It is difficult to grow within companies that have not created a culture of inclusivity at all levels, and this "dead end" leaves many women of color looking for new jobs.

RECRUIT, ATTEND, CARE, AND EVOLVE CAN BE THE
FOUNDATION FOR ANY ORGANIZATION THAT WANTS TO
CREATE A CLIMATE OF INCLUSION.

In several organizations, the climate is not inclusive. Women of color are excluded from information-sharing opportunities and social events where they have the chance to build long-term connections. As a result, they feel left out even in strongly team-based environments. No two women of color are the same, even if they appear similar. They all have different needs. When managers lump them in with everyone else without considering the individual, workers are demotivated and lose interest in their work. Generally, women of color get less of the mentoring and sponsorship vital to career development. They typically cite managers who don't highlight their contributions in front of others. As a result, these women of color are left out of the "informal networks that propel most high-potentials forward in their careers."

Recruit, attend, care, and evolve can be the foundation for any organization that wants to create a climate of inclusion.

TAKEAWAYS

"A truly equal world would be one where women ran half our countries and companies and men ran half our homes." This quote by Sheryl Sandberg says it all. When the work culture finds ways to filter out inequities actively, everyone will have a fair chance to be successful. Such workplaces will be the labs where the vaccine for gender bias can be developed. The need to be nurtured and cared for is the most profound human need and must be applied from the beginning step of hiring. This process requires vision and support from the top and push from below.

SELF-REFLECTION EXERCISE:
SURPRISING YOUR LIMITS

1. What is the highest point you aspire to in your profession?

     _____

     _____

     _____

     _____

2. Do you apply every time there is an opportunity to rise?

     _____

     _____

     _____

     _____

3. How do you plan to keep yourself updated on the latest developments in your field?

     _____

     _____

     _____

     _____

4. Are you able to attain a work-life balance with your growth?

     _____

     _____

     _____

     _____

5. Do you have a plan to share your knowledge, skills, and experience with others?

     _____

     _____

     _____

     _____

CHAPTER 6

SEEKING YOUR SAFETY NET

MENTORING AND SPONSORSHIP

"A leader takes people where they want to go. A great leader takes people where they don't necessarily want to go but ought to be."

— Rosalynn Carter

Moving to a foreign country can be intimidating. It is even more challenging when you start a new job there. One of the biggest challenges is overcoming the cultural barriers that arise. You find yourself in an unknown position. People who speak a different language are surrounding you. You face many cultural shocks before understanding the customs and traditions of that particular country. You have to go through the process of learning about your surroundings from scratch. It takes a lot of time to adjust to a new environment, and you often feel people will not be able to connect with you. But once the cultural barriers melt, you will slowly realize the similarities between you and your new community.

Being different by no means signifies that you are any less than the rest of the team or vice versa. We tend to feel overwhelmed in new settings. Stepping out of our sanctum is not easy for any of us. We are so accustomed to the rules and regulations from where we come that we do not think twice about it. However, you have to be a lot more cautious when you move to a different country and begin to learn a new way of life. It takes time to get accustomed to the norms there. Some may even experience a culture shock. Still, when you get an opportunity that seems like a once-in-a-lifetime thing, you want to grab it.

Culture plays a significant role in our lives. It recognizes every place uniquely. We sometimes categorize objects, linking them with a particular country. For example, many people will associate pasta with Italians and curry with Indians. Some may think this racist, but let's not deny that these perceptions help us explore other countries—even if the exposure is minimal.

My first job as an immigrant in the United States was in the small town of Lewiston, Idaho. I was intrigued by the new place and new position as a traveling physical therapist. It was my first opportunity to work in the field here, and my curiosity won out. I decided to take the leap.

I still remember my first day on the job as if it were yesterday. I walked into the office, and my supervisor waved me over. He gestured for me to take a seat, and I sat in front of the desk. He was with a patient at that time.

"Hang tight," he said as he waved and walked away.

I remember how confused I felt at that very moment. I did not know what I was supposed to do. I was new to the country and had minimal knowledge of American slang. I knew English well, but the language of a culture is unique to its people. So I wondered what he meant when he told me to "hang tight." I thought he had asked me to hang on to something tightly, but I did not know what he wanted me to do? I still remember the panic I felt as I immediately called my husband to help me sort it out.

Puneet's response caught me off guard. "All he means is for you to wait," he said as he laughed his head off.

"Oh!"

I remember how I felt at that very moment. It made me feel like I should have known that expression somehow. This incident is not an example of a language problem. I passed English with flying colors. I cannot blame my very British Wren and Martin English, either for my ignorance. It was just a cultural expression I had to experience to learn. I realized that most Americans used slang throughout their day. It was not just me being ignorant, either. I was simply unaware of the expressions, and I slowly had to learn new ways so I could adjust to the new environment. I doubt I will ever forget my first day at that job.

Don't get me wrong; I liked the place. The shallow pool of rehab employees had led to many travel position opportunities across the United States. Since my employer urgently needed a physical therapist, they were very supportive from the get-go. I received a tour of the nursing home that day from my supervisor. My goal was to become familiar with my workflow and my role. I was also trying to understand the work expectations. I listened to him carefully. Then he ended the conversation with a straightforward statement. "All you need to do is be a great PT and stay productive." He said it as if it were an easy thing to do. I knew how to be a physical therapist, but I had no clue about the rest of the situation, and I wished he had elaborated on what he meant. I also wished I had the awareness to ask him exactly what he meant so I could get the clarity I needed.

Moving to America posed many challenges. I had no idea how medical billing worked, or how I should document my services "appropriately" to avoid denial of payment. In India, I used to run an outpatient clinic with an average of thirty patients in five hours with just one extra technician to help set up and clean up. In my mind, that's what productivity looked like in practice. I had to do more and get paid more—or so I thought. I had to learn everything from scratch. In my new position, I realized that I needed to unlearn my previous work learning. That sounds bizarre, doesn't it? I was surprised by this insight, but I had to comply if I wanted to stay there. That's how it was. If you're going to fit in, you better conform to your new workplace's ways to avoid being left behind. I had to start my experience from scratch again. It was like pressing a reset button at the peak time of your life.

When I returned to my desk and settled my effects, I decided to make a list of things I needed to start working on immediately, so I did not feel as alienated as I had at that moment. I put cultural awareness at the top of my list because I realized how crucial it would be to service delivery and productivity on the very first day. I needed to learn about cultural differences and how vital they were.

After all, I could not keep calling Puneet every time I didn't understand something. While listing the things I needed to improve, I realized I needed a mentor to succeed. I looked around the room and saw the only other female in the rehab department. She was a speech therapist, and luckily, she was an amicable person who greeted me openly. I told her about my "hang tight" incident that morning, and she giggled. I chuckled along with her before I asked her for help. She told me not to worry about it much and that she would help me out. The next day, she brought me a list of American slang sayings. Suddenly, I felt so warm in that new unknown place. I still have that list with me to this very day.

Since my workplace was in a remote town, it had a greater majority white employee population than metropolitan cities. I sought help from the available pool. I reached out for help. I share this incident so you will understand that being in an environment without diversity or an inclusion plan does not mean you can't find a mentor. There will always be someone willing to help when you face problems. All you have to do is reach out for their help and watch them take on your request with a friendly smile, just like Kanchan did when I was visiting my parents in India. This time it was my turn to ask. After all, we all can learn from each other, can't we?

I learned a lot about my profession from that first job I had in the United States. The most striking lesson for me, which was hugely different from my prior work experience in India, was that it was not mainly technicalities I needed to learn from my American mentor. It was "how to include myself in simple day-to-day activities and be a part of them through conversations. These experiences showed me that a person should always know how to communicate appropriately in the workplace because poor communication may affect them. Communication helps you deliver services effectively; it also helps create connections that can have a profound influence on your career. To make those connections, you need to ask yourself several questions.

1. Have I introduced myself to my coworkers/clients when I meet them for the first time?

2. Have I tried to say and remember my coworkers/colleagues' names correctly without asking for nicknames?

3. Am I a patient listener when people are speaking to me?

4. Do I remember to smile when I see someone in the corridors?

5. Have I asked my coworkers/clients about something they enjoy doing in their spare time?

6. Have I asked or found what my coworkers/clients value most in life?

7. Have I indicated how anyone can help me best at work?

You can only reach your full potential if you keep learning with every step you take. Learning should be a continual process, and it does not end with starting a job or achieving your goals.

Sometimes, our egos stop us from learning because we are afraid of looking foolish in public. You will always feel like a foreigner if you do not take the first step and learn no matter where you are. Do not be afraid of asking yourself and others about things you do not understand.

As Tamuna Tsertsvadze said, "Questions are never foolish. Stupider are those who never ask anything."

I knew how important communication was, especially in a professional environment. A communication system starts with just taking the initiative wherever you are.

The real challenge for women of color lies here. With their peers being in the minority within top management, how do women create the connections that allow them to grow as leaders? How do they gain the skills and support to move up the ranks? How can they reach their optimal positions if they are unable to connect with their peers or clients?

The answer is not as simple as we all thought, and we need to delve deeper into the conversation of connection before we can come to any conclusions.

The first step toward reaching out is to identify the flow of communication in your workplace. In many cultures, finding help for work-related issues carries a similar stigma to seeking counseling. For many women of color, seeking advice on inclusion issues is virtually unheard of, even though they may feel alienated. There is a tendency to "do it all with a smile and never let them see you sweat." This tendency can be a suitable coping mechanism but not a good leadership behavior.

CLOSING THE GENDER GAP IN MENTORING AND SPONSORING WILL HELP IN CREATING CONNECTIONS.

Closing the gender gap in mentoring and sponsoring will help in creating connections. Therefore, it will boost retention rates for all women. But how can we develop deep and meaningful relationships between racially and ethnically diverse female populations at work to achieve the goal of collective advancement?

I will refer to my example. I initially took a thirteen-week travel assignment to kick-start my career in the US. But I ended up extending that an additional nine months. I eventually signed up for a permanent position—with a signing bonus—and moved to Seattle without losing working hours in transition. I was hired as a permanent employee because I was actively involved in improving my work experience and planting the seeds of career growth. *I played a role in my retention.* Others may not be able to replicate this course of action in every situation where women of color struggle to overcome barriers and biases. Still, it offers a clue to how we can achieve success. Keep your search for connections alive.

We need mentorship programs designed for women of color, by women of color. These programs should cultivate a culture for self-identifying leadership skills, addressing and customizing solutions for the mentee's specific needs, and providing tools to help mentors and mentees foster a culture of equity in their respective work environments.

The View from the Top

When you see a woman climbing the ladder that looks like you, it's natural to feel a sense of connection. You feel as if you can empathize with them on a higher level. Meeting Washington State Senator Mona Das[26] was one such experience for me. I felt a sense of belonging after I met with her.

Mona Das was born in India, just like I was. Her parents immigrated to America's rust belt with only six dollars in their pockets, and yet they were full of hope about building a better life for their family. At that time, Mona was just eight months old. She spent her childhood moving around due to her father's job. She ended up living in eight states and three countries. She finally settled down in Kent, where she currently lives. She is incredibly proud to represent the forty-seventh legislative district as a Washington State Senator.

Mona graduated from the University of Cincinnati with a bachelor's degree in psychology and earned an MBA in sustainable business from Pinchot University. She also attended the Women's Campaign School at Yale University. Mona operates her own mortgage company, MOXY Money, and spends part of her time as a leg-

---

26. Senator Mona Das, Washington State Senator. Retrieved from: http://sdc.wastateleg.org/das/.

islator. She has centered her political career on sustainable development, equal access to housing, and empowering marginalized voices.

Elected to the Washington State Senate in 2018, Mona now serves as the vice-chair of the Senate Housing Affordability and Stability Committee. She is also a member of the Senate Transportation Committee, the Senate Financial Institutions, the Economic Development and Trade Committee, and the Senate Environment, Energy and Technology Committee. During her first year as an elected official, Mona worked tirelessly on behalf of the environment, affordable housing, and equity, and inclusion.

I bumped into Mona while attending an event for a leadership program for women in Washington. Though I had met her previously, I did not have the opportunity to tell her about my book. We struck up a candid conversation about the need for mentorship and sponsored programs for women of color in leadership to help other women like us. You would be surprised to learn how many women of color struggle to understand things that are almost natural for most Americans.

Once we got comfortable with each other, I asked, "So who was your mentor?"

Mona replied with unparalleled exuberance that left me totally inspired. She said:

Let me tell you my story. About four years ago, I took my dog for a walk, who apparently had more energy than I did. I saw a sign on the roadside saying Elect Pramila Jaypal for Senate. I knew right away that it was an Indian name. I stood in front of that sign and cried for almost five minutes. I thought to myself, if another woman from Indian origin can do it, I can do it as well. The idea to run a race for the senate had dawned on me several years ago before I saw that sign, but suddenly it started feeling like it was possible. I asked the universe to help me prepare for running my race, and here I am. When I decided to run, I was an overachiever and had done five different training programs to help me run. I knew how I looked, and I knew I did not have the luxury to file for the race and just go for it. I had to go above and beyond to prove myself. There were significant allegations against my opponent. I was surprised that I still had to give an intense fight. I won by a narrow margin of 1,000 votes. Thanks to my community, who could identify with me and vote for me. I went to people of every faith and origin and asked for support.

I did not easily let anyone off the phone until I could raise a decent amount for my race. Trying to fundraise as a woman of color is an art. You need to earn faith first. That is a big hump. Many people don't support candidates of color because they think they have a reduced chance of winning. But you can generate confidence in one person at a time. It happens with persistence. It happens when they can connect to you. I knew I could do it, but I had to teach myself this art. It's like trying to help others while helping yourself balance. It is beautiful when the effort to change the world and the effort to improve ourselves align.

Mona's insight helped me in understanding struggle in achieving leadership for women of color. I realized that it required facing my fears and rating my abilities. She helped me see that I couldn't stand for fair representation of women of color unless I could be evident in my purpose and willpower in my daily life.

What's the Difference Between a Mentor and a Sponsor?

Every individual needs a network of champions to succeed. This network includes mentors and sponsors. One of the main tools successful people possess is the ability to make connections with those in positions of power. The people around us can create influence, and they may support or hinder our growth in one way or another.

THE PEOPLE AROUND US CAN CREATE INFLUENCE, AND THEY MAY SUPPORT OR HINDER OUR GROWTH IN ONE WAY OR ANOTHER.

The people with mentors have an advantage in advancing their careers due to:

- Higher likelihood to succeed since they are more prepared.

- Better job longevity and may stay with their organizations longer due to more job satisfaction.

- Better performance in their field.

- More influence on their work environment.

- Better innovative and creative skills.

- Higher resilience when they face setbacks and tend to form a more robust network.

However, people tend to confuse the terms mentor and sponsor. While both mentors and sponsors guide people and help them grow professionally, a vast difference exists between them. Below, we'll take a few minutes to look at the differences.

Mentors

Mentors are experienced individuals who are present at any level of the social ladder. Their main goal is to guide in making career choices. Both mentor and mentee drive this form of relationship.

Mentors should be responsive to the needs of their mentees whenever they need something. The mentor's primary purpose is to help the mentee determine their path for meeting specific career goals.

Mentors listen to their mentees so they can give direct, honest, and constructive feedback. A mentor may also be a sponsor, but the main difference is sponsors do more than teach and advise.

Sponsors

Sponsors are advocates in a higher position within your organization. They use their influence to help their sponsee obtain high-visibility assignments. The sponsor can choose to advocate for a sponsee, which includes supporting them behind closed doors with other leaders. Sponsors can become the champions of your potential.

Sponsors actively take part in the advancement of an individual's career. They connect sponsees to other networks and recommend them for higher positions. They push their sponsees to take on challenging assignments, so the sponsees can actively advance their careers.

Sponsors need to have some level of authority within your organization. They are most likely part of senior management. However, according to statistics, most people in upper-level positions are male. Sponsors may be important for men, but they are especially crucial for women.

Mentorship Goals for Women of Color

Finding a mentor can be a challenge, but the more significant problem is to find one you can trust. Just showing how to do a "good job" is not enough when the goal is to create an equal pitch. Mentoring is not separate from overall institutional objectives. It should not be viewed as an "add-on" but aligned with the organization's diversity and inclusion objectives. The following are some important common goals mentors must try to achieve in regards to women of color:

1. **Visibility:** Amplifying the profile of women of color concerning workplace opportunities, promotions, decision making, and so forth is vital, so women of color can move forward. There is no shame in addressing the barriers and creating a plan to help with a vested interest.

2. **Talent Retention:** Adopting strategies and tools to give women a sense of belonging within the organization is vital to advancement and retention.

3. **Regular Engagement:** Providing women of color with an environment that keeps them intrigued and engaged. It can be through small presentations, hosting a discussion panel, or creating a skill lab. The idea is to provoke regular interaction. This tactic will help in integrating the intersectionality of culture, work, and life and minimize isolation.

4. **Healthy Relationships:** Creating a collaborative atmosphere guaranteeing high-quality connections. This is important because it is one of the reasons for the leadership gap, as reported by many experts.

5. **Strategies for Thriving:** Developing strategies for upward growth and overcoming helplessness, especially when they are new to the environment.

6. **Mental Health Management:** Providing counseling for sponsees, mentees, and workers to help them cope with psychological issues like stress.

7. **Career Growth and Development:** Offering equal opportunities for growth and promotion. Enabling access to resources and information equally.

8. **Sustainable Community for Leaders of Color:** Cultivating a sense of community for the participant's professional and personal development. This outcome is the most critical.

Moreover, mentorship should be used as more than a vehicle to increase opportunities for women of color and support women of color once they arrive, thus encouraging longevity in their chosen field. It might seem challenging to find a mentor, but you will quickly realize how much people genuinely want to help you out of the goodness of their heart if you overcome your insecurities and ask.

Remember, don't be afraid to ask questions; that is the only way you can truly learn.

WHERE IS SPONSORSHIP FOR WOMEN?
THE IMBALANCE

Having a mentor and sponsor is essential for progressing in your career. However, an imbalance exists in sponsorships between men and women. Men are more likely to be sponsored because sponsors can also get a little biased, and since most senior managers are white men, they tend to identify with and reach out to people who look like them. Therefore, we need to add diversity to upper management.

So, what causes a low likelihood for women to find a sponsor? I will discuss a few reasons below.

- **Man to Man:** Men often tend to gravitate toward other men when it comes to sponsors. They are most comfortable with "their kind." They see in another man the same potential they possessed at some point in their career and genuinely want to see others progress in their careers as they have. It is human nature to be attracted to those who are like us in some way. We often feel a sense of tenderness when we come across someone who reminds us of ourselves. Men have no qualms about being sponsored because they see it as another step in their careers.

On the other hand, women tend to feel uncomfortable when it comes to asking someone to sponsor them to climb the organizational ladder. The power structures remain unchanged because sponsorship for men is much higher than women, even without other factors, such as being biased and making assumptions all by themselves. Most sponsors hesitate before taking a woman under their wing as they weigh their options—unlike when they decide to take other males under their wing. Almost every other sponsor makes assumptions about women's capabilities and interests rather than asking them directly about them. Instead of helping them reach a higher level, they start making decisions for them, assuming that a woman cannot make career choices like a man does when traveling and relocating. Another assumption is that the travel schedule will be too much for women because of their children. These notions can become the deciding factor whether or not they deserve a challenging position. Nobody speaks aloud about these assumptions, but they are ever-present in the backs of their minds, which only hinders a woman's success at work.

- **Role of Bias:** Throughout history, leadership has fallen predominantly to men, despite how cultures have changed over time. We all learned history in school. The majority of the past is about wars, battles, or expeditions of one culture over another. At that time, yes, men played a significant role because of their physical strength. From media to literature, men represent leadership, while women present the supporting role. We have a long history of male leaders and automatically assume men are better at it. Competent women are struggling under the leadership of males. I doubt that the males holding majority leadership positions are more qualified. Let's face it—women have a lot of historical, political, and religious baggage to overcome in a world built on brute strength and testosterone. To clear away some of the stereotypes about themselves, women spend half their lives under stress and have grown accustomed to it by the time they start their careers. Women have fought tooth and nail to get into industries dominated by men. Women are just as capable of handling the stress of new challenges. We need to tackle bias and put the idea of women being less behind us. Because at the end of the day, regardless of gender, we are all human, and every human is capable of handling challenges if given a chance.

- **Women in Power:** Women in high-level positions advocate for other women; however, their advocacy comes at a higher cost. More often than not, women in top posts are penalized with lower competency and performance ratings whenever they step up to advocate for women and diversity. That is why they hesitate before sponsoring other women with potential. On the other hand, no one reprimands a man when they take the same step and are even rewarded for supporting diversity. Women positioned at a higher level must take this risk with all these odds. If they don't, then we will continue to face gender bias and discrimination when it comes to the workplace. Organizations should mitigate power and prejudice. To do so, both men and women in powerful positions should mentor and sponsor talent regardless of gender.

Sometimes women tend to believe that someone will notice them if they do an excellent job at work. They most likely think they will be able to reach promotion if they do it all by themselves. My only advice to such women would be not to do it alone. Keep the search for a sponsor active, and every person in the working field should at least have a mentor who can guide them through the ups and downs they face in an organization. Without access to mentors or sponsors, you will take longer than you anticipate and may never be able to overcome challenges that arise in the progression of your career. It is imperative to create a network of people helping you to advance in your career, and the only way you can do this is by having a sponsor by your side.

TAKEAWAYS

Mentoring and sponsoring are essential, particularly for women of color. It is a proven fact that successful leaders need a network of winners, including mentors and sponsors. Self-advocacy is a must for women if they want to move their careers forward. But to succeed, no one can do it alone. If women don't have access to the relationships critical to recognizing them and advancing their careers, they will miss out on cracking the ceiling. And, in fact, women are missing out.

It is time that workplaces prioritize mentorship for women, which can help them navigate their careers. This effort will lead to a visible shift in perception by senior leaders because they will have a higher chance of seeing women's skills and potential. Establishing a mentoring or sponsoring relationship has the potential to remedy the leaky pipeline of talent.

SELF-REFLECTION EXERCISE:
SEEKING YOUR SAFETY NET

1. What qualities would you like to seek in your mentor?

_____

_____

_____

2. Did you ever have a mentorship experience? Was it helpful? Are you still looking for a mentor?

_____

_____

_____

_____

3. Describe a scenario where your performance was affected because of a lack of support and guidance.

_____

_____

_____

_____

4. How do you think you communicate when you need help?

_____

_____

_____

5. Create a list of resources where you can network with people to support your journey.

_____

_____

_____

_____

CHAPTER 7

RESTRUCTURING EMPOWERMENT

BE THE CHANGE

"We cannot all succeed when half of us are held back."
— **Malala Yousafzai**

I have seen it often when people donate money with the intent to support women's empowerment programs in Third World countries. According to many people I interviewed, the common belief was that a small financial amount is enough to empower a woman, allowing her to buy pieces of equipment like a sewing machine and start a small business with it. Monetary contributions are the most common assistance I have encountered for women's empowerment. There may be different ways to donate money to women around the world, but the objective behind these donations remains the same: to empower women. However, women's empowerment is not just an economic issue globally; it's much more.

A well-harbored myth exists that the best way you can help a woman in a developing country is by donating a few dollars. As women, we need to come together and help other women progress in their countries to achieve the freedom of working or running their businesses there. Believing a simple act of "sponsoring equipment" by a benevolent Western donor can change a woman's life is a misguided form of zeal for empowering women.

Often, we forget as allies for women that our role is like a tool women can use to exercise control over their lives. The focus of empowerment should be activism against discrimination, which can prevent choices and opportunities to reach women. The even bigger issue is the fear instilled in the women that makes them avoid speaking up for themselves and puts them in second place in household or social conversations.

OFTEN, WE FORGET AS ALLIES FOR WOMEN THAT OUR ROLE IS LIKE A TOOL WOMEN CAN USE TO EXERCISE CONTROL OVER THEIR LIVES.

Unfortunately, several women from my background, who have shared their experiences with me, have experienced this fear. They don't have choices regarding their careers or personal matters. They deal with outcomes of barriers posed to them. They sometimes have to work when they are least prepared. Many people in this world twist the meaning of empowerment around to suit their needs and goals when they are reaching out.

More often than not, women themselves misuse the term empowerment, which only spreads misinformation regarding this effort for equality.

What Has Gone Wrong with Empowerment?

The Fourth World Conference on Women[27] held by the United Nations in 1995 adopted an agenda for women's empowerment when 1980s feminists introduced the term empowerment in connection to women. Empowerment is mostly applied to ending gender subordination. It also is expanded to political and social realms.

Decades later, the word empowerment is defined as "the granting of the power, right, or authority to perform various acts or duties."[28]

Therefore, it can be expressed as a term that includes a sense of ability and power.

So, if I use myself as an example, I would feel a sense of *ability* if my manager gave me a project to lead at work and gave me the tools to do it. However, hat empowerment may not be enough unless I also feel a sense of power to use the tools effectively. So, without proper mentoring and training to champion it, I may still not be able to make much difference for myself. Thus, people who feel creating opportunities is enough for women's empowerment may not succeed fully in their efforts.

In a different scenario, my manager at work asks me to take charge of supply reimbursement. He gives me access to the funds to execute the task. I will get a sense of *power*, but if I am not provided with an opportunity to build my ability to deal with policies and processes, the effort of that empowerment may be futile. Thus, people who believe that donating resources to help is enough will fail in their attempts at empowering women.

This loud cry of "empowerment," which gives women positions of power without the skill to succeed in them, now serves every-

27. The United Nations Fourth World Conference on Women. Retrieved from: https://www.un.org/womenwatch/daw/beijing/platform/plat1.htm.

28. Merriam-Webster. (n.d.). Empowerment. In Merriam-Webster.com dictionary. Retrieved July 8, 2020, from https://www.merriam-webster.com/dictionary/empowerment.

one except the women it is supposed to help. The concept behind introducing empowerment was to validate the struggles faced by women daily in their professional and personal lives. The main objective was to root women into positions of power and exercise their fundamental human rights without opposition. It was supposed to provide them with a sense of security when it comes to standing on their own feet.

FOCUS OF EMPOWERMENT MUST BE ON
WAYS TO PROMOTE INDEPENDENCE
AND FAIRNESS.

Handing out a donation may help the women in Third World countries achieve a way to earn income, but it focuses more on providing them with things than assisting them in obtaining their own. I have seen First-World feminists and global development organizations pointing to the empowerment they brought for marginalized women in the rest of the world. I have witnessed them flaunt success stories of their efforts at conferences and various social media outlets. I have observed development professionals point toward training sessions, workshops, and spreadsheets laden with "deliverables" as evidence of another successful empowerment project. However, I believe that in their ideologies, there is little room for the complexities of the recipients. Women affected by society's inequities must not be reduced to mute and passive subjects awaiting rescue. It's time to make empowerment meaningful and thoughtful. Development organizations' programs must be evaluated based on whether they enable women to increase their potential. They need to be assessed in a way that allows them to create sustainable gender equality.

The concept of women's empowerment needs an immediate and urgent rescue from the clutches of the would-be saviors in the development industry. At the heart of women's empowerment lies the demand for a more robust, global sisterhood, one in which no woman is relegated to passivity and silence. The voices of women speaking up about their issues, ranging from sexual harassment to discrimination in pay or hiring, need to be amplified.

The #MeToo Movement

Women's voices are stronger than ever. The modern world can witness the magnification. Countless examples exist of women excelling in letting most people hear their voices. Many global movements bring the ugly truth out into the open: Women are oppressed irrespective of which world they belong to. It is an uncomfortable truth, and it is unpleasant enough to place people in denial. No one is ready to accept that most victims in the world are females. Women and children are at the top of assailants' lists because of their vulnerability. The entire #MeToo Movement took the world by storm as it revealed horrific events that take place in many people's lives behind closed doors. More often than not, the predators are people who are close to the women—be it at home or work.

Women involved in raising awareness through the #MeToo Movement have rightly received the praise they deserve for breaking the long-held silence about workplace harassment. It has opened up the suffrage roadshow of how many women hide behind a hard exterior. The problem some people have with twenty-first-century women is they are no longer afraid of speaking up and letting their voices out. For centuries, women have suffered countless types of abuse at some point in their lives. Only a small percentage of women around the world were sheltered from it. Women who suffered through it were told to remain quiet, and their traumatic experiences were hushed down because no one was ready to hear about the trauma they went through. They were told to be meek or face utter humiliation by confiding in people. However, times have changed, and women are tired of holding themselves back from fear of being judged. Women are no longer going to be subjected to victim-blaming when they are harassed.

Women are speaking up about sexual harassment and decrying the wage gap in industries from entertainment to technology. Their voices are finally being taken seriously. This welcome development is long overdue.

Many people believe the #MeToo Movement started on October 15, 2017. On this day, Alyssa Milano asked Twitter users to write "me too" as a response to her tweet if they had experienced sexual harassment or assault at some point in their lives. This request opened up the gates of sexual abuse that women and men were subjected to during their lifetimes. Although it spread like wildfire in social media at that time, it was first initiated in 2006 by Tarana Burke. She is credited as the founder of the "Me Too" movement. She began using the phrase "Me Too" to raise awareness of the pervasiveness of sexual abuse and assault in society. She wanted to connect to people who experienced sexual assault and wanted to do something to help women and girls. Her efforts were particularly for women and girls of color—who had also survived sexual violence. Burke has mentioned in several interviews a girl named Heaven in Alabama, who told Tarana about her sexual abuse by her mother's boyfriend.[29] Tarana didn't know what to say to her, and after that, she never saw the girl again. She has expressed that she wished to say "Me too" to her. Burke formed a belief that girl's issues were distinct from those of their male peers. Her experiences and observations led Burke to found Just Be Inc., an organization that promotes the wellness of young women of color aged 12–18. Tarana and her organization have worked tirelessly to help young women create a foundation that allows them to be creative, inspired, resilient, patient, confident, and kind. The organization wants the girls to know that when all else fails, they are equipped with everything they need to "just be."

This is an interesting example of how a decade of work by a woman of color was amplified by the viral hashtags of white women. However meaningful the hashtag has become, it will take more than a hashtag to do the real work that is needed now in every corner. It astounds me how selective racism occurs even when it comes to a topic as dark as sexual abuse and workplace harassment. Take the following example of a street harassment analysis.

According to numerous statistics, women are harassed on streets in abundance compared to men. The number who daily experience this form of harassment is shocking, but it has mostly become a thing of the past. It is about time we realize that cat-calling or harassing strangers on streets, especially young boys and girls, is globally unacceptable. It is especially important to understand this sort of behavior is abnormal and needs to be condemned as quickly as possible to prevent sexual harassment from becoming part of the norm.

29. https://www.washingtonpost.com/news/the-intersect/wp/2017/10/19/the-woman-behind-me-too-knew-the-power-of-the-phrase-when-she-created-it-10-years-ago/.

No one, indeed, looks into details until we can't look away. Now that women have taken the initiative to speak up for themselves to raise awareness, the next step is even more difficult. It requires resilience and tangible actions. Every cause needs work to sustain hope.

EVERY CAUSE NEEDS WORK TO SUSTAIN HOPE.

MYTHS THAT HOLD US BACK

The next step after raising awareness is increasing women's active participation. It is a challenging step for various reasons. The need to tackle this challenge is vast because women are entering the workforce and becoming entrepreneurs or independent consultants in higher numbers than ever before. Women must be represented equally in ratio to men at the highest levels of our business and government institutions, where real changes can be made. Women are equally earning degrees in professional courses, but they remain a distinct minority in the uppermost positions.

WOMEN ARE EQUALLY EARNING DEGREES IN PROFESSIONAL COURSES, BUT THEY REMAIN
A DISTINCT MINORITY IN THE UPPERMOST
POSITIONS.

We have all heard the clichés that feed the myths. The most common myths are that women avoid risks and that discounts their leadership ability. This bias creates a sense that women need fixing, not the situation. Focus is needed on how inequity is affecting women and evaluating the models of empowerment. This will definitely promote efforts to strive for communities where no one is held back. Together we can eradicate the myth that empowerment can be done just through giving things or finding out what women are lacking. Here are some of the most common myths I have I want to review:

Myth: Women's Empowerment Makes Men Less Relevant

In the so-called "good old days," women had fewer rights. They hardly had any opportunities to have economic independence. Even physically, women were supposed to be protected by men. Men were the saviors, knights in shining armor with their innate instincts to guard women. In the modern era, the word chivalry evokes a kind of old-fashioned male respect for women. But during medieval times, the code was established for much starker reasons. Gallantry was a construct to protect fragile females from violent and predatory men in the world. The idea behind gender roles was that a female was complimentary to a male. Women and men were seen as radically different. It was best to have strictly assigned tasks for society to function.

In the last few decades, women have gained a plethora of rights; women have access to birth control, education, and economic opportunity. The increase in power and independence for females has led many to question: Should men continue to be like a brave knight who protects women when women insist on being able to take care of themselves? The most significant benefit of the traditional ways was that a man could have his ego and self-esteem boosted by knowing he was needed by the fragile, delicate, and vulnerable women. The females in his life had to rely on his strength and principles. The orthodox warn that women who exercise "too much" sovereignty over their lives can make men feel irrelevant. According to them, men who feel irrelevant will have a poor sense of commitment and will behave irresponsibly about everything, thinking "woman will take care of things."

But the opponents of progress are wrong.

Leaving aside their wrongness on the more significant questions of women's autonomy, they are wrong about men. They are mistaken in their insistence that with female vulnerability, men will have the onus on responsibility. Still, without it, men will invariably descend to a level of aimlessness and recklessness. Over the centuries, societies have raised men to believe their worth is contingent on how well they take care of vulnerable women. The cost of traditional gender roles undeniably has exacted an enormous price from men. Under no circumstances should a man only be viewed as someone who has the privilege to guarantee safety and happiness. Men must not be trying desperately to play the part of protector and provider for women generation after generation. Therefore, women's empowerment has liberated men as well.

WOMEN'S EMPOWERMENT HAS
LIBERATED MEN AS WELL.

Feminism, in regard to many new and exciting roles for women, offers men a chance to rethink their worth and purpose. It provides them with an opportunity to be intimate allies with their female partners. It allows them to build relationships based on more than duty and reliance. It gives men a chance to be valued and loved as the whole person they are, rather than solely for what they can provide.

Feminism does not make men less relevant or threaten their position in society in any way. It merely gives them the chance to represent themselves in a better stance as more than just women's protectors.

Men are people too, and their personality runs deeper than only the chivalry society had beaten into them for generations. The entire problem lies in a centuries-old trained belief to respect a woman if she is sweet, frail, and soft-spoken. Girls who are outspoken, confident, and independent could be viewed as "bad women" in some males' eyes because they could not fathom that women could live and survive without men. How can they survive without men when we have told them that every girl needs a protector in her life? This change does not sit well with men who still have not evolved from the old school of thought, so they start opposing women who do not want to live as inferior beings but equal beings. We women do not want to be respected based on the context that we are someone's sister, daughter, or mother.

We simply want to be viewed as equal partners who should be recognized because we are individuals. We women are more than just our gender. We are thinkers, explorers, believers, and adventurers, just like men.

We simply want to be equal every day and everywhere.

If equality in gender is compromised, men can become overprotective or completely narrow-minded. No one wins in this situation. When we women demand our rights, we are not demanding that men should step down. We want to elevate their sense of self. We want them to discover their true selves while we still fight to seek freedom for our existence.

Myth: Women Need to Change

It is easy to blame women when it comes to problems. We blame women whenever they are harassed, or we pass their complaints off as them being oversensitive. "It's not that bad" is said sometimes to issues of harassment. "Take it as a compliment," some may say if it comes to pestering women on the street. According to some people, it is always the woman's fault for being attacked in any way. Whether it is mental or physical abuse, our minds mostly try to come up with an excuse for why the victim deserved to be treated that way. According to these people, the list of things women need to change keeps getting longer.

- Change the way they dress to avoid coming off as provocative.

- Change their tone to timid and lower their voices.

- Change the way they wear makeup to come off as less inviting.

- Change their clothes and cover themselves more.

- Change the way they stand out.

And so, the list goes on as society tells us to change, change, and change! Aren't we all too tired of hearing this narrative over and over again? Why is it that only women are required to change?

Why can't we simply teach the difference between right and wrong to our little boys? Why can we not tell boys it is rude to stare? Why can we not tell boys and men to stop viewing girls and women as a "distraction" for their existence? Why is it that women need to change and not men, who have been thriving off their antics longer? Why are we teaching our girls to be more careful? We know how the world functions, and we know what kind of predatory men and women lurk in the dark. And yes, women can be predators as well as men. The sickness of the mind does not see gender when it comes to infecting their thoughts. Every one of us is capable of doing bad things. The only thing that holds us back is the moral code and ethics taught to us since childhood. Instead of asking women to change, why can we not change the environment we have created for ourselves?

There is another myth that talks about women avoiding conflict. We crack under pressure. We don't take risks. We lack confidence. We are too emotional—the myth piles on the reasons to explain how women are the weaker sex. This myth falls apart when you change your perspective. We all need to expose ourselves to the winds of change to be equal. It is the way the system can be repaired so women can thrive uniformly.

> WE ALL NEED TO EXPOSE OURSELVES TO
> THE WINDS OF CHANGE TO BE EQUAL.

Once the perspective is changed across the globe, the awareness will prevent anyone from being blinded by society's narrative, and it will be a common understanding that women are more than just the titles with which they have been labeled. When it comes to leadership, women have the necessary leadership skills. We have what it takes to lead and execute that role awesomely. But the way we lead may be different from the way men lead. When it comes to self-improvement, we all have room. So the spotlight should be on our perspective that needs to be freshened up.

Myth: There Are Not Enough Qualified Women

Look around yourself and notice how many women you see in the workforce. You will see women employed in many companies. A higher percentage of women graduate from college compared to men. Women make up 46 percent of the workforce.[30] So why is it hard to believe that companies around the world cannot find enough qualified women?

In many cases, unqualified men are chosen instead of qualified women because of unconscious bias. It is not about the pipeline; it never was. Men are given more importance and chances during an interview because people often automatically assume they are supporting their families. Women who walk in for an interview often lack visibility because of the bias.

We simply need to develop our female and male employees equally. Instead of being biased about who deserves a certain position within an organization, we need to decide who is more capable of getting a promotion based on their merit. We should be grooming both sexes for advancement by tackling the bias during recruitment.

Myth: STEM Is for Men

Technology is the basis of our lives in modern times. But there is a well-known myth that women lack the skills and aggression to succeed in the field. It's gender bias, rather than ability, that turns women off STEM (science, technology, engineering, and mathematics). You don't have to go very far to find women who are living examples of reprimanding this myth. The truth is that stereotyping threatens the success of women in the field of technology. If technology is not a woman's thing, then why are there women working in the STEM fields?

Here is the list of women who were not only a part of STEM programs but excelled greatly.

---

30. https://www.weforum.org/agenda/2018/01/myths-holding-back-women-workplace.

Dorothy Vaughan[31]

You may have watched the movie *Hidden Figures* based on Vaughan's story. Vaughan was a female mathematician who worked as a human-computer at the National Advisory Committee for Aeronautics (NACA). NACA was later transitioned into NASA. She belonged to the segregated group of African-American women at Langley Research Center who solved complex mathematical calculations by hand. She had specialized in flight paths, the Scout family of rockers, and FORTRAN computer programming. She became the first black supervisor at NASA. She taught programming language to women so that they could prepare themselves for the transition and ensure they would not lose their jobs when computers would replace them. Dorothy Vaughan was the image of strength.

Kitty O'Brien Joyner[32]

Kitty O'Brien Joyner was not only one of the first women to graduate from the University of Virginia's engineering program, but she was also the first woman engineer at NASA. She initiated a successful lawsuit so she could be permitted to receive her education at a time when women were barred from enrolling in an all-male engineering school. She operated as an electrical engineer at NASA for thirty-two years. During her career, she managed several wind tunnels, including supersonic wind tunnels. She used to test new aircraft designs before they would go for a flight. Her contributions as an engineer are critical in defining the standards we have for modern aeronautics today.

---

31. Hodges, Brian. (2017). Learning from Dorothy Vaughan: Artificial intelligence and the health professions. Medical Education. 52. 10.1111/medu.13350.

32. Kitty O'Brien Joyner. NASA. Retrieved from: https://www.nasa.gov/langley/100/kitty-obrien-joyner.

Nancy Grace Roman[33]

Nancy Grace Roman is identified as the "Mother of Hubble." She was the first female executive at NASA. She earned her nickname for making contributions in the planning and setting up of the Hubble Telescope program structure. She also developed and budgeted various programs and helped in launching three orbiting solar observations and three small astronomical satellites. She made multiple discoveries while she worked as an astronomer. She paved the path for other women who wanted to become a part of NASA.

Kalpana Chawla[34]

The example of Kalpana Chawla personally takes me. She was the first woman of Indian origin to go to space.[35]

She obtained a degree in aeronautical engineering from Punjab Engineering College in India before immigrating to the United States. She earned her master's degree from the University of Texas. Later, she was honored with a doctorate in aerospace engineering from the University of Colorado in 1988. The same year, she joined NASA's Ames Research Center working on power-lift computational fluid dynamics.

In November 1977, she had her first mission and was part of a six astronaut crew that flew on the space shuttle *Columbia*. Chawla became the first Indian woman to fly in space. For her second mission in 2000, she was a mission specialist, but that mission got delayed till 2003. She died in a tragic accident on February 1, 2003, while reentering the earth's atmosphere. It was a heart-wrenching, and the second-worst space disaster in history.

---

33. Dr. Nancy Grace Roman. https://www.nasa.gov/image-feature/dr-nancy-grace-roman-astronomer.

34. Kalpana Chawla: Retrieved from: https://spaceflight.nasa.gov/shuttle/archives/sts-107/memorial/chawla.html.

35. Space.com.

Chawala was posthumously awarded the Congressional Space Medal of Honor. Several universities, including the University of Texas named their school departments after her. In her own words, "When you look at the stars and the galaxy, you feel that you are not just from any particular piece of land, but the solar system."

Kalpana left a legacy for everyone. But above all, hope for women to lead in all sectors no matter where they come from.

These are only a few out of thousands of exemplary women who worked in the field of technology. Not only did they work there, but they made several discoveries, we still do not know about today. Everyone knows about Neil Armstrong, the first man to walk on the moon, but no one knows about Margaret Hamilton,[36] the former director of the software engineering division at MIT. She was the one who designed the on-board flight control software on Apollo spacecraft. But we never read about her achievements because the history textbooks only talk about the first man who walked on the moon, not the woman who made the moon landing possible.

Myth: Meritocracy decides who gets the work

"Gender bias is not a problem in the modern world. Even if it is, it does not affect hiring decisions or in owning enterprises." I have heard this over and over in diversity-related conversations. A study by the National Academy of Sciences[37] makes it apparent that implicit gender bias affects women's promotion and hiring.

In this randomized, double-blind study, 125 science faculty hiring managers were sent identical resumes for a laboratory man-

36. Margaret Hamilton. https://science.nasa.gov/margaret-hamilton

37. Corinne A. Moss-Racusin, John F. Dovidio, Victoria L. Brescoll, Mark J. Graham, Jo Handelsman

Proceedings of the National Academy of Sciences Oct 2012, 109 (41) 16474-16479; DOI: 10.1073/pnas.1211286109. Retrieved from: https://www.pnas.org/content/109/41/16474.

ager job. They rated the application materials of a student—who was randomly assigned either a male or female name. The result breaks the myth that women have an even pitch when it comes to careers. The male and the female evaluators ranked resumes with women's names as belonging to people of lower competence, who were less recruitable, and lacked appeal as potential mentees. The discrimination didn't stop at hiring. Salaries offered to females who landed the job were, on average, $3,500 lower than those provided to males. An unconscious bias led the evaluators to favor men in this case.

A new study published in *Nature Human Behaviour*[38] talks about results based on actual academic hiring data. This study says that committees whose members don't believe that gender bias exists are less likely to promote women. The evidence suggests that when people recognize that women might face barriers, they can check their own biases.

The study considered actual decisions from forty hiring committees who filled elite positions with France's National Committee for Scientific Research over two years.

The prejudiced perception that a small number of women in mid- to upper levels of management or business is due to individual failings or lack of availability in the market means we ignore the effects of unconscious bias and subtle and structural discrimination.

Myth: Women with children are not serious about careers

It is a well-observed fact that women's child-bearing years overlap with a critical career period. Many people believe this is an insur-

38. Régner, I., Thinus-Blanc, C., Netter, A. et al. "Committees with implicit biases promote fewer women when they do not believe gender bias exists." *Nat Hum Behav* 3, 1171–1179 (2019). https://doi.org/10.1038/s41562-019-0686-3. Retrieved from: https://www.nature.com/articles/s41562-019-0686-3.

mountable disadvantage that can make women underperform in their careers. This belief has another consequence: If women are trying too hard in their careers, then avoiding motherhood is better.

Haven't men and women always had children?

Then why must women face this myth?

Frankly, I "want it all" as well. No, don't assume I am asking for any special treatment. When it comes to balancing career and family, I am willing to take on more than my fair share of the work involved in having both. But I have known that it is hard. Women can plan motherhood or decline motherhood as a choice more freely than ever. But for women who go with the option of raising kids during their peak career years, it is an area requiring focus and improvement. Despite the efforts of major companies to provide flexibility and offer paternal leave for men, it's still a quandary. We can advocate all we want, but it is a predicament. If we are gone for a short time or a day or several days, the notion will be that we choose motherhood over careers. This prejudice led to added stress levels for me during my early career years, and it still does. When I moved to the United States, it took a while before I was offered a job. I was almost thirty. I began to feel a sense of urgency to plan my family, due to the ticking biological clock. My example has social and cultural expectations wrapped in for women to bear kids by a certain age. I gave in to those norms. I was working for about a year when Krish, my first child, was born. I was fortunate to have a great employer and received my FMLA, which covered a few initial weeks of maternity leave. But returning to work was not as simple as I thought. I always was running late to work due to waking multiple times at night to feed my baby. I always looked tired. I felt drained too.

I was working in Seattle, which was twenty miles from our newly bought home. That commute felt tough, so finding a job closer to home became more lucrative. I quickly switched jobs, switched my schedule to Tuesday through Saturday so that Krish had one less day in daycare because Puneet was available on Saturday, found good backup care for Krish, went to work early, and came home at 5 p.m. sharp, working through lunch to save time. The weekends were all devoted to family time, playing with Krish, birthday parties, or playdates.

I felt lucky that I could do all that quickly to make it work. More importantly, I was not alone; Puneet helped me. I am sure for many women that finding that flexibility to switch work or schedules or find a suitable backup or be able to return home on time may not be as simple. I realize how much harder it can be if they are working as a single parent.

I have observed in my interviews with working mothers that most of them don't feel impressed with solutions or examples to balance work and life. The maternal wall is real. It has layers and layers of interconnected issues, which can lead to forced sabbaticals to raise families, settling for lower pay and lower expectations for their career. Until more concrete solutions are available to counter this wall, women will continue to struggle with solutions to find the critical balance of working motherhood.

Myth: Barriers faced by women are uniform

Women's experiences differ vastly in terms of social, demographic, economic, or cultural context. Every aspect can bring its own set of barriers. Then why are the problems faced by women treated as a uniform set? Many obstacles, such as lack of access to resources, missing financial support, insufficient social protection, and women's unpaid work burden, exist across the globe.

Many women of color have to deal with racism in addition to sexism and ageism. I call it "*age-ndered racism.*" I have pointed out various examples in this book of how there are significant disparities for women of color, generally salaries in all sectors and representation in leadership roles. There is a need to home in on their work experiences in every industry. Although there has been more emphasis on race and race equity in workplaces and every other career platform, there lies a need to see how those efforts have played out for removing unique barriers for women of color.

Myth: Women don't want to be on top

Data says that women are represented at entry-level almost equally, but their numbers fall to one-fifth of C-suite executives. An assumption exists that this shortage at the top is due to a lack of ambition. This myth has been proven wrong, according to CNBC and SurveyMonkey's new Women at Work survey.[39] They surveyed 1,068 working US women and found that 54 percent said they are "very ambitious" when it comes to their careers. A substantial percentage said they are "somewhat ambitious." Just 3 percent said they're "not ambitious at all." This scarcity at senior leadership points to the many ways men experience acceleration and advantages in their careers in comparison to women. Inadequate representation in senior roles is not just an inequity issue but also a critical business issue. Trillionscan be added to the country's economy if gender parity is reached by next 5 years. There is a need for strong policies and procedures that can safeguard women's career paths to advancement to bridge the leadership gap.

---

39. https://www.surveymonkey.com/newsroom/cnbc-surveymonkey-women-at-work-survey/.

TAKEAWAYS

Initiatives and programs not well informed regarding hidden barriers will only focus on telling women what they should do to succeed. The revolutionaries will ask them to do whatever they want. Neither approach is entirely accurate. Positive change needs a balance of courage and common sense.

POSITIVE CHANGE NEEDS A BALANCE OF
COURAGE AND COMMON SENSE.

It's not fair to expect women to be able to find their way out of systemic problems. The experiences of women of color range from being ignored and overlooked to less mentoring on the job to "hypervisibility," meaning they are under the microscope for every decision they make, and they deal with biased assessments. The higher pursuit is needed to invent solutions to address multilevel and organizational barriers. Once women can navigate these barriers and biases, the foundation for more resources, training, and advancement opportunities will become more beneficial on purpose. The circle of empowerment can then eventually complete.

SELF-REFLECTION EXERCISE:
RESTRUCTURING EMPOWERMENT

1. Reflect on a situation where you were best able to use your ability and power to achieve your desired results.

   _____

   _____

   _____

   _____

2. Do you feel your abilities sometimes do not match your responsibilities?

   _____

   _____

   _____

3. Do you feel you lack the power to use your talents completely?

   _____

   _____

   _____

4. What have you done in response if you have faced or witnessed harassment in any form?

   _____

   _____

   _____

5. What is your plan to bridge your abilities, power, and courage to benefit you and your professional environment?

   _____

   _____

   _____

   _____

CHAPTER 8

DISCOVERING AND BUILDING YOUR MALE ALLIES

FEMINISM IS FOR EVERYONE

*"Human rights are women's rights,
and women's rights are human rights."*
— **Hillary Clinton**

The quote above is one of my favorites. It was delivered by then First Lady Hillary Clinton at the United Nations Fourth World Conference on Women in Beijing twenty-five years ago. A quarter-century after the Beijing Platform for Action was adopted in 1995, no country in the world has achieved gender equality. It's unfortunate that in many countries around the world, gender bias still takes its toll and has almost come to the point of decimation by law. In many nations, women still face legal discrimination based on gender.

This chapter is for men who want to take on this challenging role but are unsure of how it works. Empowerment is not just a woman's issue. Men are equally responsible for and a part of this journey, even if women lead it. This book is more than just a march toward liberation. It is a march toward fundamental human rights—rights that have been taken away from women for as long as anyone can remember. But together, we will break the chain.

You may believe that no one can discriminate against women in the modern world by law. You may also theorize that gender inequality today has more to do with social impediments than legal ones. For example, as discussed in this book, companies paying a new female recruit less than the salary negotiated by her male peer, or women doing more unpaid work than their male partners are both scenarios occurring due to the prejudice of a few people, but the law protects us as entirely protected by law.

You would be wrong.

I want to draw your attention to the recent World Bank survey, Women Business and Law report 2020.[40] This report has assigned an index to identify legal obstructions to women's economic opportunities. The goal was to track *legal* equality between men and women in 190 economies. This report measures the formal laws and regulations governing women's ability to work or own business at various stages. The focal points range from the basics of transportation to the challenges of starting a job and getting a pension.

The study recognizes the uneven path of advancement for most women:

- The majority of countries surveyed still had at least one law impeding women's economic opportunities. Only the high-income countries scored best, leaving women in many countries with only a fraction of the rights of men.

---

40. https://wbl.worldbank.org/en/reports.

- Women face gender-based job restrictions in many countries, often confining them to low-paying activities leading to income disparities.

- In several countries, women are withheld by marriage since the law gives husbands the authority to restrict their wives from obtaining work outside the home.

- So far, only eight economies score fully in terms of legal equality between men and women. They are Belgium, Denmark, France, Iceland, Latvia, Luxembourg, Sweden, and Canada.

This year's study (2020) covers the last fifty years. It reports undeniable progress over the years in closing the gender gap, as women increasingly entered the workforce and started owning businesses. The dramatic gains were primarily seen in the ability of women to start a job.

Still, gender barriers persist, and laws and regulations continue to restrict women's economic decision making and employment prospects. That's truly unacceptable. Women should be as free as men to pursue their dreams. They should get the same pay as men for work of equal significance. The discrimination must stop when women are interviewed for a job, apply for a loan, ask for a raise, or start a business. Women should have the same rights to own property and inherit as men. Legal rights for women ensure fair societies where all can thrive, and they are valuable from an economic perspective too.

Research has proven over and over that reforms and policies that empower women boost economic growth. When women have freedom of movement, are able to go to work, and can manage their income and assets, they're more likely to join the workforce and strengthen the economy. Technology is making women well connected to business opportunities around the world. No, legal obstacles must not be allowed to stand in their way. That's not just because it's economically smart. It's because discrimination shouldn't be by the law.

MORE THAN 2.5 BILLION WOMEN AND GIRLS ARE AFFECTED IN MULTIPLE WAYS BY DISCRIMINATORY LAWS AND THE LACK OF LEGAL PROTECTIONS.

According to UN data, when you look around the world, more than 2.5 billion women and girls are affected in multiple ways by discriminatory laws and the lack of legal protections.[41] This fact is heartbreaking. We are entering the third decade of the twenty-first century, and it is time. We need to look hard at what progress has been made over the years. We need to review the practices embedded in and the laws that govern our societies, and how they enable or hinder the rights of women and girls. Observation should lead to assessments, and that must, in turn, lead to plans and action. Around the world, there has been remarkable work to address inequity based on gender. But any initiative depends on both men and women to successfully join hands, share experiences and expertise, and exercise their social, economic, and political will to achieve meaningful and lasting reform in uplifting the status of women and girls globally. Together, we can pave a much-needed transformation. Together, we can get closer to the goal of delivering equality and empowerment for all women and girls.

Women make up around 50 percent of the world's population and a little over 50 percent in the United States. Women can and

---

41. https://www.unwomen.org/en/digital-library/publications/2019/03/equality-in-law-for-women-and-girls-by-2030.

should be at least half of the workforce, and even half of the leadership. Every day I go to work, I see myself surrounded by brilliant and talented women. They work as hard and aspire as much as their male colleagues to work their way to the corner office. But unlike their male peers, they cannot move forward because the pipeline is leaky, and not many men will step in to help shoulder the burden women have forever carried.

People often ask me, since I am a mother of two boys, why I am still such an advocate for women. Wouldn't this make men secondary? I always have the same answer; I am responsible for my sisterhood, who face the same challenges as I do because of the broken system, and I have an obligation to help my boys understand and acknowledge the importance of equality in the household and professional world. I want my boys to step up and take the central role in the conversation.

> I WANT MY BOYS TO STEP UP AND
> TAKE THE CENTRAL ROLE IN THE
> CONVERSATION ABOUT EQUALITY.

Even when I was waiting for my sons' arrival in the world, I envisioned for my sons: compassion, good citizenship, excellent college educations, successful careers, and achieving whatever they strove for in their lives. Also, I wanted them to be feminists like their dad.

So the question I want to ask men is: Does it take much to be an advocate for women?

Let us ask this of the men in our lives. I know the answer is no. The hardest part of male advocacy is to discover how to be an advocate. I have talked to many men who were very willing to be the warriors of gender equity but uncertain how to do their part to help. Knowledge is vital to ensure progress. I will make sure I do my part. I intend to continue to raise my boys to respect women and be champions for women and girls' initiatives. I hope that I can provide some tools and knowledge for advocacy in my pursuit. My efforts will continue to entice and convert more male advocates. The big picture is to create an even pitch to ensure everyone's daughter has an equal opportunity to become the next CEO, governor, or maybe even break the world's highest glass ceiling—President of the United States.

Many people have a hard time accepting that women are demanding fundamental human rights. The very rights they have been deprived of by social norms over centuries. Most men want to run away from the truth because it is easier than admitting their silence over centuries. I suspect some even do not want to relinquish the power and privilege that comes with dominating society.

What does it mean to be a male advocate for women's rights, in deed?

In a 2016 survey by *The Washington Post* of the current wave of feminism, only one-third of men reported identifying as a feminist.[42] Why so few?

Is it because we're not cheering men into this combat as much as we should be?

Could it be that men genuinely don't know what feminism is?

Are they uncertain about how they can contribute?

---

42. https://www.washingtonpost.com/graphics/national/feminism-project/poll/

Are men browbeaten by other men when they call themselves feminists?

Whatever the reason behind the lack of male advocacy, I believe it's a battle where everyone counts. Today's generation embraces feminism in its own unique way. The need is to explore how men are taking the mission of equality and making it their own. How are they expressing feminism? Are their actions more an online sprawl of dialogues than a political mission led by activists?

We need both men and women to play a role in contributing to global change. History has proven time and again that working together on women's issues reaps groundbreaking results; for example, during the women's suffrage movement, women fought alongside male advocates to win the right to vote.

I believe that for every prejudiced male, there are several men who aren't biased and are searching for ways to educate themselves and contribute to female empowerment. I salute men who believe in gender equality, equal pay for equal work, and equal advancement opportunities for women when it comes to senior-level positions or similar support for women entrepreneurs. Their role is essential toward creating a fair representation of women in all areas. For men interested in becoming more involved as male advocates, the time is now to fix the leaky talent pipeline before losing the best candidates for leadership positions to systemic barriers.

My husband often shares in social situations his thoughts on how masculinity needs a new meaning. In many warm, personal talks, he has shared his effort to reconcile who he is with what the world expects of him. According to him, "the qualities you pack in the mold set by gender roles, strength, bravery, and toughness need a new definition in the modern world. The perception around qualities must change from good man to good human. Let's define strength with sensitivity. Let's define bravery with humility. Let's define toughness with empathy. Men who can cry when they are hurting are not weak. They should not be bullied like they are sissies. A confident man is one who doesn't feel threatened with equality. A man who is willing to listen to women in his life with respect and value should be a norm, not an exception. Men must not feel attacked when women are sharing their agonies from experiences with other men. They must offer to understand and prepare themselves to confront men who cause any form of harassment. Keeping quiet is not enough anymore when you hear other men flaunt any misogynistic behavior. It takes courage for women to speak up, especially about what they have experienced due to inequality. As a man, the care and compassion in your heart must never be undermined by the historical shell of masculinity surrounding it.

KEEPING QUIET IS NOT ENOUGH ANYMORE WHEN YOU HEAR OTHER MEN FLAUNT ANY MISOGYNISTIC BEHAVIOR.

"Women's strength is an excellent complement to caring men, and both need to be harvested for gender equality. Men must not be shy about asking for help to break the molds because the goal is togetherness, not seclusion. Both men and women have a lot to learn to create an equal pitch. Be prepared to witness a mess up and strive to do better. Be ready to hear the wrong thing and learn to correct it. Be ready to get offended and help to fix it.

"Use hope and a positive mindset to promote fairness. In general, I believe that men will rise in purpose more than ever as we continue to build and share the world's dream without discrimination. This vision can only be achieved through allyship. The examples we set for our future generations are equally important. Let's not just raise brave boys or good-looking girls but fair and good humans."

Dialogues like these help generate an insight that we have many male advocates among us who may just need to be highlighted and educated to help amplify the voices of feminism.

The whole idea of women's empowerment is to let the world know this is not just a woman's problem; it is a human problem, which means it is not restricted or limited to women. It is a universal problem that needs to be tackled together.

I Tried It at Home

When I had Krish, my first child, I felt alone. Puneet was busy working as a senior manager at Microsoft and often brought his work home. He was so busy sometimes that I had to make sure he didn't miss his dinner. I started developing an opinion that maybe men are not good multitaskers. He often tried to help out whenever possible, but we were not much connected as a couple. I had to figure out a lot on my own. We had just bought our new house, and Krish was born within a month of moving in. Everything around me just felt out of place. My in-laws were in town to help me with the new baby, but I wondered what they would think of me since that house was not me, and I was not myself. Puneet and I seldom spoke, and if we did, it was only about mundane things to run the household. What hit me the most was we didn't seek to get on the same page to where we were heading.

Suddenly, it dawned on me to ask at that stage of my life, "Who am I?" I used to be a full-time rehab clinician and a wife; now, I was a mother with a young child and an executive husband who had no time. This insight pushed me harder to find balance. I discovered that the missing theme in my life was to have a partnership at home, which works in *all* circumstances. It didn't necessarily mean we should divide everything equally and push our struggles aside. It didn't mean sameness. It meant having a voice. It meant honoring each other's preferences. It meant sharing power. That's when I began my uphill climb toward *equal partnership* at home. I found out Puneet wanted it too, but we had to go a long way before we understood exactly what we wanted and the steps we needed to make it possible.

> I DISCOVERED THAT THE MISSING THEME IN MY LIFE WAS TO HAVE A PARTNERSHIP AT HOME, WHICH WORKS IN *ALL* CIRCUMSTANCES.

Having a partner in your life is fantastic, but creating an equal partnership at home is a skill we all need to learn. And there are no tailor-made solutions. It's a seesaw between two where you find your balance by bouncing back and forth. Puneet had to learn how to be equal by giving room to my perspective, and I had to learn how to speak up instead of judging and dismissing myself. We had to figure out a lot about each other. We had to understand who could handle what better; for example, if I am good at maintaining social relations with friends and community, I will manage that without being opposed by Puneet; if Puneet is good at investments, he will do more of that without being challenged by me. But what about matters where we had a difference of opinion and strong convictions? This happens to everyone, and if we can't learn to honor our spouse's preferences and listen to them respectfully, then even simple matters can turn complicated. We discovered how to handle it gradually. But most importantly, we learned it *together*.

By the time I had Vansh, my second child, we were on the path to equal partnership. I was finishing up my doctorate at that time, and Puneet was busy with his Microsoft job as usual. Our families started saying, "Now, after wrapping up your degree, you can focus entirely at home with the baby while Puneet is busy with his job." Frankly, that's not what we wanted. So Puneet and I discussed it and agreed that I could start applying to work as soon as I felt ready. This decision cemented our partnership. Reflecting on it in retrospect, it was a great decision. I got the opportunity to serve as director of rehab soon after, while we both shared household responsibilities reasonably well. If we had not understood the value of equality in marriage, we would have been living in separate worlds; we'd have had a physical presence but no mental connections. We would have felt like we didn't have a voice or influence, making us resentful and angry with each other. We may have been equal in performing our separate duties in our marriage, but we would have lacked companionship or partnership. One reason we both were sold on the idea of equal partnership was that we had role models in our lives: our parents who have modeled ways to nurture their marriages.

Earlier, I discussed unpaid work. It has always affected women more profoundly than men and causes a shift in power that so acutely disfavors women because it gets deeply embedded in the fabric of society. Our parents broke the mold of just being spouses in the marriage. They demonstrated the hard work they did to keep each other happy, the pride they felt in honoring each other's requests, and the time they took to hear each other out with their "What do you think?" phrases. They modeled enthusiasm in marriage by *sharing* unpaid work.

Understandably, some people struggle more than others with sharing power at home. One possible reason is how we were raised. For example, if you have been raised in a strict environment where you have to follow many rules and your opinion is not heard much, you may develop a passive approach in your personality where you just go with the status quo. On the other hand, if you are raised in an easy-going home, then you will get lots of attention and freedom, which can make you uncompromising. Our tendencies can affect our marriage or partnership. The only way to break a pattern of behavior is to identify it and question it *intrinsically*. It has to come from *you*.

Until I asked the question, "What am I doing? Why am I so alone?" I could not find the path to build an equal partnership, and I created an *ally* in Puneet to walk on it with me.

CURRENTS OF CULTURE CARRY
THE WAVE OF CHANGE.

Why Should Men Advocate for Women?

I don't believe change can happen with only one person or one couple a time. Currents of culture carry the wave of change. To create those currents, we need to stir the stories and bring them to the surface. That's why I am sharing mine. Also, I don't want to project that I know it all when it comes to finding solutions to equality. I had a good set of challenges and flaws. The truth is, I learned more by sharing them.

I was puzzled initially when I heard of male advocacy and wondered how men could help in issues that affect women. So, it is essential to explain why male advocates in a professional environment are crucial for their female peers.

Male advocates are essential for two primary reasons:

1. **Men Are in the Majority:** Whether we like it or not, most people in formal and informal positions of power are men. Anyone can deny this all they want, but the truth remains unchanged. Men have a great deal of influence and hold significant decision-making places in the world. When it comes to leadership in any sector, men are better positioned to impact the dynamics than most women. Advocacy by men in powerful positions can help women advance in crucial areas too. Just verbally acknowledging that girls and women face discrimination will not stop the perpetuation of those forms of oppression. Men need to be in solidarity with women and girls in their daily struggles.

2. **Equality benefits men too:** I have stated previously that equality is not only a women's issue. It is a social issue and a cultural issue that includes all. As a result of these matters, there is a lack of women representation in key positions. It becomes even more crucial when we add the lens of race to gender. Equality is beneficial for men in modern times. It translates to balance and fair opportunities. The equal relationships, either personal or professional, tend to be more meaningful and lasting. At home, they can manifest as effective parenting practices and better-functioning children. At work, they can prove to provide more positive interaction and outcomes. It can also mean a better range and retention of talent, which can enrich professional arenas.

So, What Should Men Be Advocating? The *New* Normal

Religion, traditions, and centuries-old practices disguise male dominance very well. We all understand how finely it got woven into "normal" culture. The heavily loaded moral question here is: For how long? I honor women who have wrangled the male monopoly in all the realms of human life. I have sincere gratitude for women who are amplifying female voices in every sphere to shape equal societies. But we can't do it alone. We are still "outsiders" in many areas, and we need "insiders." We need male allies as the agents of reform.

My question to men is: Which side do you choose to stand on when women raise questions about the fairness of systems? Do you wish to be next to women to challenge the rules or barriers? Or do you choose to remain silent about practices you know are wrong and discriminating? No matter what you say, the answer lies in your actions.

- The primary focus of male advocacy is not all about helping specific women or protecting them. You may appear condescending or patronizing for women, even if you are well-intentioned. Men can start improving the workplace environment to help women feel safe and assured when presenting their ideas. Why do I say so? Because a large body of evidence indicates that communication behaviors are often gendered. When a person talks in groups, it adds to their perceived influence. Women are interrupted more frequently than men. Mansplaining and microaggression are just a few of many issues that can affect workplace pitch. Communication may appear a trivial matter, but how we communicate tells other people how they are valued. I am sure you will agree with my understanding that when anyone is appreciated, they will likely feel like they belong as much as others in that environment.

- Men need to advocate for systemic change as much as women. Many straightforward ways exist in which men can break biases they see taking place by speaking up against them. If you believe certain women deserved promotion and are being overlooked, you can step in and vocally state it straightforwardly. Many women who are often ignored and forgotten do not see any point in speaking up for themselves because they are afraid of being passive-aggressive. Instead, they leave the matter alone to save themselves the trouble of being labeled something that can affect their mental wellbeing. Male advocates can be fair and give women credit where it is due. The role of male advocates is not to *supplement* female voices but to set the stage and amplify it.

- Intervention for individual instances may not be enough to change the person in a commanding position, so the best way is to also advocate for altering systems. This advocacy includes eliminating subtle bias in job descriptions, interview practices, performance evaluation criteria, flexible work policies, and task assignment patterns. These systems have developed over time around the majority group's needs, but they are now proving disadvantageous, particularly for women. The norms that created these systems did not include women or minorities since forever. This change can be more daunting and may even appear unfavorable for men, but do not let it discourage you. Making systemic changes can be advantageous for both men and women and create an equal footing within the organizational structure.

The Challenging But Crucial Business of Male Alliances

Below is a discussion of the challenges male advocates face frequently:

1. "I don't know where to start?"

Conversations around barriers against women in any area can never be natural. Male advocates might come across many challenges. It is vital to work toward equality, but it's more important to address the subtle and hidden biases that prompt stereotypes, prejudice, and, ultimately, discrimination. The only way a man can understand what a woman goes through in her professional setting is by listening to her side. Often, many well-intentioned men try to bring systemic changes without really understanding or listening to what women want in their careers. Listening to women's problems is crucial because it can create a sense of understanding. Often the difficulties presented by women get misunderstood due to lack of attentive listening. This inattention can lead to ill-informed advice. Men need to sit down with their female colleagues to understand what they are trying to tell them. Doing so can help develop a deeper understanding of the issues at play here to figure out how to address these issues. It is easy to jump to our conclusions if we don't have this level of understanding, so men should avoid giving misguided advice to their female colleagues. Intentions matter, but the way you convey your intentions matters even more. *Attentive listening* to a female colleague's problem is the first step toward understanding what barriers exist in the environment around you.

2. "Not all men understand advocacy."

I have heard men convey that there is no need for male advocacy because there is no such thing as women's issues in the modern world. My suggestion to male advocates trying to fight this apathy is to start by focusing on influencing people who are more open to your efforts. Like that mantra in business, you want to focus 80 percent of your energy on the best running units and only 20 percent on problem ones to succeed. Men must emphasize their focus where they are likely to win more allies. Of course, with a more compelling atmosphere and data, you may be able to win over the less-interested category.

3. "Some men need more compelling discussion before they can act."

Sometimes advocates face the challenge of lack of awareness around gender inequity issues. It's a problem of inadequate information. Everyone has their way to receive knowledge, and one size does not fit all when you are sharing it. The best approach is to share information in the way it can reach your audience. I have put together a list of resources at the end of the chapter, including tips to increase advocacy awareness by providing the right information in the right way.

4. "Some want to help but don't always know where the problem lies and what to do about it."

When you lack clear reasoning, it becomes challenging to advocate. Take the example of a scenario where HR has shown up at your workplace and provides a condescending discussion of equity but fails to give data about where the problem lies and what is recommended. Will you feel you got the logic? The same scenario can exist with everyone as a team going into an open discussion with the company's leadership and reaching an agreement about the values of your organization. It will analyze how company culture reflects it; doesn't that become an impactful rationale and prompt an action? Advocates need to reach *all levels* of the workforce or decision-makers to buy into the effort. It is also equally essential to provide, share, or create resources as a team to carry out actions.

5. **"I encounter the common belief that it's majorly a social problem, and the workplace cannot solve it."**

This statement reflects a lack of suitable examples for how creating a culture of equity in organizations can affect the issues of gender and racial inequalities—any success, however small, counts when you are trying to include women in key positions. Therefore, quoting examples within your environment or beyond is very helpful to visualize how, despite considerable social barriers, coordinated efforts in small pockets can be pivotal in minimizing gender and racial divide.

6. **"I fear a negative experience with advocacy."**

We all have felt this whenever we step in the door of being an advocate for women. These initial fears are related to the risk of facing pushback. Sharing other men's successful experiences as well as worries is a significant step to reduce concerns. The best way to tackle the issue is by possessing a growth mindset. A growth mindset stresses that characteristics like intelligence and the ability to improve ourselves are innate or inborn. These areas can be improved with effort and practice over time. We can hone these skills like a sharp sword, so any hard impact does not mellow it. Having a growth mindset is just a shift in how we perceive negativity in our lives. Either we can give up on the idea of being an advocate or learn from it and come out better than ever before.

7. "Where to find the time?"

Often, I have encountered people willing to help, but who can't act on anything. Time management is a personal issue and a real one, too. In today's fast-paced lifestyle, finding time can be hard even for the most committed advocates. One way to face the challenge is to have a few short terms and measurable goals compared to a bigger purpose. It helps to stay accountable and lessen the impact of time constraints.

8. "Lack of support at the top."

Sometimes, you hear cordial words, but that does not translate as help from the leadership team. It is critical to receive support from senior leadership in the form of commitment and resources to bring about cultural changes. This area can be a challenge if you see it lacking in your environment. My suggestion is to start with small steps. Try to identify people who are open to the conversation regarding advocacy. It's worth trying to win support even if it's only one executive in the top team. Showcasing even little successes can be an effective way to kick-start strategies necessary for equality and to minimize the leadership gap for women.

9. "Equality is often talked about, but practices do not reflect it."

To challenge is to ensure the action. Several organizations do not provide sufficient time for paternity leave. Many new mothers have to resign from their jobs due to the unseen complications that arrive after the birth of a child because the fathers cannot offer them the support they need. These natural factors are frowned upon and make female employees less reliable in their employers' eyes. Most women are lucky enough to get a sufficient amount of time off to recover and bond with their babies, but what about fathers? Having paternity leave is a rare gift in itself in America, but it is not a common benefit. According to Federal law, the Family and Medical Leave Act grants fathers or secondary caregivers up to twelve weeks of unpaid leave. However, the majority of fathers only take around ten days of leave—if they take any at all. Most fathers miss out on bonding with their children because they are expected to put in the same hours and efforts they did before the child's birth. Many organizations view fathers who take paternity leave as lacking professional drive and commitment. In the end, even men are stigmatized by paternity leave. Male advocates must not only seek the courage to speak up about their female coworkers, but to speak on their behalf in terms of the unfairness they face based on the bias when it comes to certain things like paternity leave and employee retention.

Active Steps for Male Advocacy

Creating a Safe Space or Listening Opportunity

Creating a safe space or listening opportunity means to create an opportunity where people can share perspectives without fear of being judged or "saying the wrong thing," which is a common concern for any group in the minority in a given environment. Male advocates will benefit the most from creating this safe exchange of stories and dialogues. Active listening is vital to avoid assumptions and take practical actions. It also helps to take great examples to make your efforts impactful. Start with someone you trust and encourage them to share their experiences. It is equally important to recognize that women, like any other group, are not homogenous, and not every woman wants to share her expertise. Even if you do not have minority experience, it is crucial to understand why women of color who are underrepresented differ in opinions and beliefs around the issue. Therefore, being aware of the difference in views can help with understanding the importance of listening and inquiring to understand where individuals currently stand on these issues.

Speaking Up

Talking about these issues with other men is an important step in challenging the status quo.

Men, take time to ask yourselves, "What is my response when I hear an offensive remark at work? Do I address it or stay quiet, hoping for someone to change the topic or do something about it?"

> WOMEN ARE OFTEN MORE INTERRUPTED IN MEETINGS THAN MEN, AND THEY GET LESS CREDIT FOR THEIR IDEAS.

When a woman colleague isn't given credit for her ideas, what do you do? If she is talked over or "mansplained" to, do you pause to correct the person? When was the last time you suggested a woman lead a particular project? Women are often more interrupted in meetings than men, and they get less credit for their ideas. These issues create a gap in their influence compared to men's authority.

It's often observed in meetings that many women tend to have great ideas, but they are left unsaid from fear of having everyone's attention in the room. Male advocates need to support their female coworkers whenever they present their ideas.

You can start helping women by encouraging them to sit in the center of the meetings. Interject whenever a man interrupts a female coworker and ask him to wait his turn. It is essential to make sure everyone speaks up and is equally heard.

Promoting Fairness

Many males tend to overestimate their abilities, and females tend to underestimate theirs. This type of bias is even more pronounced when reviewing criteria is unclear, and managers rely solely on "gut-feelings."

Most women are less likely to apply for a job if they meet all criteria except one. They easily give up and overlook the application, deem themselves as unworthy of the position, and move on to the next application. However, men are more likely to apply for a job even if they do not meet all requirements. Do you see the opposite effect that criteria have on men and women? Men are often daring and get called for an interview based on potential. Men are hired and promoted based on potential, whereas women are hired based on their accomplishments.

MEN ARE HIRED AND PROMOTED BASED ON POTENTIAL, WHEREAS WOMEN ARE HIRED BASED ON THEIR ACCOMPLISHMENTS.

That is why male advocates need to make sure every person on their team is aware of unconscious gender bias when evaluating performance. Unconscious bias occurs when our preexisting beliefs and attitudes subtly influence our behaviors, affecting our decisions. Micro-inequities often result from unconscious bias. It is subtle gestures and expressions that can make a person devalue themselves or discourage them from striving further, leading to withdrawal and passing up opportunities. Awareness of this fact begets fairness. Many men take both small and big steps to confront the gender bias around them. The effect is magnifying if it comes from men holding key positions. Therefore, I stress the need to question each other whenever the idea of "gut feeling" comes to decision-makers' minds. This checkpoint is crucial to avoid biases while evaluating women.

Influencing Likeability

Many times, women are viewed as "mean" and even rude when they reach a successful level. This trade-off between success and likeability may be directly proportional to men, but it is indirectly equivalent to women. Many successful women are disliked by their peers, which creates a double bind for them. If a woman is competent, she is viewed as a problematic person. But a congenial woman is often considered as less qualified. Many successful women have to accept that they are disliked due to their successful status. This fact also has a considerable impact on women's careers. Ask yourself who is more likely to be supported and promoted—the man with excellent credentials, or the woman who has equally high marks but is disliked by the majority for being competent? Women have to deal with this bias when it comes even to leading teams. They are often viewed as bossy whenever they simply assert themselves. When a woman promotes her ideas, she is seen as aggressive and ambitious. When a man supports his opinion, he is seen as confident and secure. These disparities are cases of perception, and it can only change by the cumulative efforts of advocates who actively fight these views on grassroots levels.

Minimizing the Pay Gap

The biggest drawback many employed women worldwide face is the gender-based wage gap, usually known as the gender gap. Many women earn around 80 percent of what white men earn, while Asian women earn about 97 percent, Hispanic women earn approximately 58 percent, and black women earn around 66 percent. Women of color also face discrepancies due to their race.[43]

This disparity is an issue male advocates need to speak up about for the betterment of women. Many employed women still live on the lower tier despite the responsibilities placed on them. They are expected to receive less in return for simply being employed in a prestigious position.

This wage gap is a constant problem for women. This narrative has existed for years worldwide, especially in Third World countries, and has cost many women the opportunity for a better paycheck. Most women seem to have closed in on the gap due to their access to college and advanced degrees. However, this is still not enough because women are required to have additional degrees to occupy higher positions. In contrast, a man with a lower degree can easily bag that position in the same organization. If we compare education with wages, we can easily conclude that women need doctoral degrees to earn the same as men with bachelor's degrees. This apparent bias in the gender gap only creates more disparities in wages, and

---

43. US Bureau of Labor Statistics, Current Population Survey.

women are still ten steps behind because of it. Male advocacy is an important initiative that needs to be implemented in more places.

User Alerts for Male Advocates

Be careful about the variety of perspectives regarding diversity equity and inclusion efforts. A great approach is to be an ongoing learner and active observer to understand where people stand on these issues. It will be helpful to explore why women and other underrepresented minorities differ in their perceptions and beliefs around these issues.

Some men may share a concern about reverse discrimination. This worry is often due to jumping to conclusions without knowing the details. An example of reverse discrimination can be when a person fears that the organization's efforts to hire more women may deny equal opportunities to men. A few may feel that they are not the ones who practiced the original discrimination, but they are now on the receiving end. These feelings of threats come in quickly. They can be combated with dialogues and discussions based on ethical, economic, and historical facts. This effort requires creating bridges of relationships ahead of time within communities and organizations to address the basis of inequities and need to fight bias.

Too much advocacy but too little groundwork can be sabotaging for women. It is crucial to make sure that women are well prepared for leadership. It is like planting a garden; too much watering will not help until we have patiently followed the right rate of growth. Similarly, accelerating women in their fields requires a balance of training, mentorship, and opportunities. Male advocates need to be careful to avoid placing women on a glass cliff. It can be a scary scenario to invite a woman to accept a challenging leadership position without appropriate opportunities to develop the skills she needs to fight the challenges. It is well researched that this situation happens often, and if the woman fails, she bears the blame of the whole. Male advocates need to carefully identify the skill set and meticulously develop training opportunities by keeping the best interests of a woman in mind to set her on a path to success.

MALE ADVOCATES NEED TO BE CAREFUL TO AVOID PLACING WOMEN ON A GLASS CLIFF.

Male advocates need to leave room for individuality while mentoring. It may be tempting to provide cookie-cutter tips and advice, but those may not be very helpful if you are mentoring women. Remember, you are not trying to create a template of yourself. A great way to keep yourself in check is to advocate for change that values a variety of leadership and communication styles. This effort will help break the mold of associating only certain traits with leadership.

In light of Working Relationships in the post #MeToo era, it is essential to understand what people are experiencing in the workplace. According to several men I surveyed, almost 50 percent are uncomfortable participating in a collective work activity with a woman, such as closed-door meetings, working late, or after work socialization with teams. This is heartbreaking to know. Now, more than ever, we need to recognize male allies and capture the actions of the men advocating for women's advancement. These male advocates can be your coworkers. They are allies who need to be highlighted and thanked for putting their beliefs and values into action.

TAKEAWAYS

I started this chapter stating that men are an integral part of the equity equation. I compiled concrete steps for how to be part of that equation, such as recognizing and examining unconscious bias and holding an open conversation about gender and fairness. Being an advocate starts with an understanding of what we believe is right and continues into how we put these beliefs into action to demonstrate our values. While disparities in access, representation, and participation in decision-making remain, we want all hands on deck working on the problem. Both men and women need to play a role in closing the leadership gap and ensuring a welcoming and motivating environment for women in various positions. I hope this chapter's discussion can help build increased understanding so we can all work as advocates together to increase diverse participation and inclusion in technology workplaces.

BEING AN ADVOCATE STARTS WITH AN UNDERSTANDING OF WHAT WE BELIEVE IS RIGHT AND CONTINUES INTO HOW WE PUT THESE BELIEFS INTO ACTION TO DEMONSTRATE OUR VALUES.

SELF-REFLECTION EXERCISE:
DISCOVERING AND BUILDING YOUR MALE ALLIES

1. What is your idea of an equal partnership at home?

    _____
    _____
    _____
    _____

2. Identify unpaid work in your life.

    _____
    _____
    _____
    _____

3. How do you plan to share the unpaid work?

    _____
    _____
    _____
    _____

4. Do you feel resistance/microaggression when you strive for equal partnership?

    _____
    _____
    _____
    _____

5. Structure a plan to identify and build male allies to achieve gender equality.

    _____
    _____
    _____
    _____

CHAPTER 9

PAYING IT FORWARD

"In the future, there will be no female leaders.
There will just be leaders."

— Sheryl Sandberg

Earlier, I mentioned that I went to a private Catholic school in India. My initial lesson in empowerment came from there. When I was in the ninth grade, my school encouraged high schoolers to engage in a literacy program for underprivileged kids as one of its projects. Behind the closed confines of schools, it was hard to understand the inequities of society. Therefore, this was a great initiative to open doors to even the most indigent kids in the neighborhood so they could come in and sit down in the same classrooms and receive primary education via enthusiastic volunteers in after school hours. When my mother heard about the program, she was very supportive of me volunteering in it. I was supposed to find the student who would benefit and was willing to come to the classroom and, in turn, be able to teach other underprivileged children of their community. My high-schooler brain was working extra hard to find an easy solution to this problem. I asked my mother if she could help me find who needed support and was willing to come in for after-school community lessons. My mom was sieving flour in the kitchen when we were having this discussion. She put down a bowl of flour in front of me, drew a line in it, and said, "*Bete* (Hindi for "my child"), there is a line that divides society into 'haves' and 'have nots.' The people above the line are going to be more okay the proportionally higher you go; the people below the line will continue to suffer the lower you go. No one will reach people below the line if they think of convenience while providing a token of help. You must always strive to reach out the farthest you can when you step up for the community." Her drawing in the flour made me understand the line of poverty. The farther down anyone is from the line, the more marginalized they get. This dialogue helped me understand the value of knowing the need and planning what resources could help. I thought if people above the line can think similarly and reach farther down to share their knowledge and resources, then the world can never forget about the marginalized population. People can be in your proximity but still be marginalized for various socio-economic reasons and remain isolated from communities.

PEOPLE CAN BE IN YOUR PROXIMITY BUT STILL BE MARGINALIZED FOR VARIOUS SOCIO-ECONOMIC REASONS AND REMAIN ISOLATED FROM COMMUNITIES.

I want to tell you about some girls who were isolated from the flow of life. I found them after I had that conversation with my mom. They worked as *dhobi* (Hindi for "laundry helpers") to cater to the laundry and ironing needs of my neighborhood, including my home. It is a challenging way to earn a living because most of them work under makeshift huts unprotected by weather extremities and sometimes in hazardous environments. When I approached them about the prospect of learning at my school in the after-school program, they were happy to see me come and talk to them. They all wanted to learn how to read and write, but most importantly, they wanted to help their kids not to end up with the same fate of hardship and poverty. What struck me most was their short sentences and referring to me as *didi* (Hindi for "elder sister," and a way of showing respect) even if I was younger than them. I found it awkward, so I asked, "Why do you call me *didi*?" They all replied, "*Kyonki aap madam Ji ki beti ho*." (You are the daughter of madame we serve). This answer still rings in my ear because this is how a social class sounds when a section of society gets marginalized and faces disparity. People consider themselves below just because of what they have to do to live. This self-image is the opposite of becoming a partner in a mission, and therefore, I felt helpless, even though I wanted to offer whatever help I could. So, I decided that even before starting after-school learning, I had to find a way to make them feel comfortable around me. So I offered them listening. I wanted to know their stories. Once we started speaking regularly, I learned a lot more harsh realities about their lives, barriers to education, early arranged marriages, lack of opportunities, and social support. I got tearful listening to each of their stories. These women were my first partners in figuring out ways to understand the basis of inequity. They faced dire circumstances, and yet they displayed incredible enthusiasm and determination to do better for their families.

During those days, I understood that when designing programs to help people from any particular community, we also need to understand the circumstances of their lives. I had never imagined that something might be more critical for them than what I planned to offer. I just thought that providing an opportunity toward literacy would be great until I realized how long their working hours were and how important it was to work daily to bring food to the table. They wanted me to find time around that to squeeze in the opportunity for them to learn. They had no time to go anywhere to learn anything else. So instead of trying to find someone else as an option for my after-school literacy program, I decided to ask them, "What time works for you?"

We figured out a late-night hour after dinner and household chores to meet up in their neighborhood and kick-start their classes. That was the plan for a few months till they could learn to read basic books. This plan worked because it came *from* them. They worked equally hard, and if one girl missed a lesson, the others would help her make up. That hour of meeting up became a safe space for them to talk to each other as well. They could share their joys and agonies and celebrate and empathize with each other. In my head, I thought I was running a small literacy program. However, in reality, I discovered something more meaningful: women from marginalized sectors of society working together to cheer and help each other move up. This project was my first lesson in empowerment.

Sharing stories helps create belonging and identify the hidden bonds. A sense of belonging develops a sense of purpose and identifies issues worth speaking up about. Speaking up creates courage to work and fight for what is right. In our little classroom, we all *felt* equal because we were all working together toward what mattered to us. Together, they all broke the myth that since they were denied literacy, they did not have the right to literacy; just because no one reached out to them before did not mean they couldn't come together and lift each other.

When Women Support Each Other, We All Succeed

Recently, I attended a leadership program in Seattle for women. I feel proud to belong to Lisa Brown Cohort, an exclusive sisterhood of the most dynamic women in Washington State—a group ready to take on the role of leadership in political positions and elevate it to new heights. Twenty-five women were in my cohort, and each woman has an amazing story to tell. They have shared with me their struggles in this journey of life and how they have had to face certain moments of truth to get where they are today. Like everyone else, these women have a dream and are brimming with ambition. They are contributing their efforts to make a substantial impact in this world. Their ability to take the world by storm motivated me to do the same. They are constantly flourishing in every stage of life, and they have accomplished so much even after facing every hardship one could imagine. They have fiercely fought for their positions in this world. They have picked themselves up even after life decided to knock them down. It takes an immeasurable amount of strength for women like us to win such positions. The best thing about being under their leadership is they do not create followers. These women go out and create more leaders by mentoring women through all stages of their careers. We all know how women lack mentors who can rightfully guide them in life. The truth is a strong woman is a great example for all women. No one can understand our problems and struggles better than another woman who has also seen such drawbacks in her life. Years later, I relived the same experience I witnessed in my literacy project as a learner in this classroom of emerging leaders of our democracy.

THE TRUTH IS: A STRONG WOMAN IS A GREAT EXAMPLE FOR ALL WOMEN.

To flourish and progress as a nation, I believe we need to see gender equality and the inclusion of diversity in public offices as well. A wise person once said that diversity is like being invited to a party, and inclusion is like being asked to dance. But I always wondered what the person who is asking someone to dance represented in this scenario. I realized it was up to my interpretation. I decided to see that person as the symbol of equity—the idea of being fair and impartial. Equity is different from equality. For example, if you go to a meeting and bring a handout for everyone to know the agenda, then you are treating everyone equally, but if you invite people to the meeting who could benefit from it and use the information to succeed but would have been excluded if you didn't make an effort, then you have practiced equity in its true essence. Equity requires deeper thought and action.

EQUITY IS ESSENTIAL FOR CONNECTING DIVERSITY AND INCLUSION

Equity is essential for connecting diversity and inclusion. It is about each of us getting what we need to survive or succeed—access to opportunity, networks, resources, and supports—based on where we are and where we want to go. The concept of equity is important because it promotes justice and fairness in society.

Leadership is a great tool for promoting equity. Women, now more than ever, are making major cracks in the glass ceiling. In the case of women of color, we are making cracks in the marble roof since barriers have many layers. It is easier to crack the glass, but it takes time, effort, and great strength to crack marble. It's only a matter of time until that gets shattered for good. I am sharing here my experiences as an immigrant woman of color in an attempt to draw some broad lessons and create a snapshot of what the leadership of the future will hold when women can emerge without barriers and biases and just as themselves without compromising their personal goals. And how they can use what they have gained to pay it forward to women who need it to succeed similarly.

I have emphasized my journey because my experiences have helped me form my views and understanding of why representation and leadership matter for all, and especially for women like me. My experiences have also shown me how everyone can contribute to cracking the ceiling.

> ### LEADERSHIP IS A GREAT TOOL FOR PROMOTING EQUITY.

One of the woman who has inspired me the most is someone I met only once in India before coming to the United States. Shubhi Lall wrote a book with my husband as the main protagonist, *Why Outside? Why Not India?* The book was basically about putting together a narrative of large-scale migration of talented and skilled Indian IT workers who have left India to work in different parts of the world due to various systemic reasons. That was back in 2003.

When I read the book, I was busy planning my wedding and wanted to learn more about my husband. When I met Shubhi, I found her warm and gritty. She asked me if I was sad about leaving India to settle in the United States, and would I be able to bring Puneet back to India. That question amused me. Coming to the United States is a dream many young hearts have, no matter how much you love the country where you are born. I never thought about whether I would be sad to leave home before she asked me that question. I guess I was too rosy-glassed with the prospect of the upcoming wedding. I said, "Actually, I have asked him if he ever wanted to return to India, and he said he plans to settle in the US."

I told her I couldn't have an opinion yet because I had not been to the US. Besides, my physical therapy profession had better opportunities in the US than India, but she cut me off and said, "If you get a chance to return to India, you have to take it."

I was stunned. Shubhi had just written a book about the challenges of professionals in India, but she wanted me to consider moving back if possible? I had to ask, "What makes you say that?" She replied, "Because your chances of making a difference are much greater here since you are from here. The US is a great nation, but India needs talent, too. It needs people with revolutionary mindsets and skills who will not leave but challenge the status quo, especially for women. If you get that chance, take it."

This was a riveting moment for me, and it's one reason I am a passionate advocate for women who are trying to make a difference in societies they were raised in rather than leaving them for good. It made me realize the importance of paying forward the kindness and hope I had received from my mentors in India.

It always excites me when I meet such women wherever I go.

Recently, on a cruise to Alaska, I had a dinner conversation with a couple traveling from Mumbai, India. They mentioned that they were visiting Canada to drop off their daughter, who was enrolled at the University of British Columbia. "That's exciting," I said. They mentioned they were very excited, too, except they were still trying to figure out how they could manage the non-profit organization their daughter had been running in India since she was young. I was intrigued. I asked them about her work and her mission.

They shared with me that their daughter, Vrisha Vyas, and her friend, Hinal Jajal, cofounded "Swach Tan Mann Paryawaran" (STaMP), a non-profit organization (meaning Clean Body, Mind, and Environment). Its mission is to help women in their community fight barriers they face to maintain menstrual hygiene. Through this non-government organization (NGO), they have been trying to eradicate the myths and taboos that exist in society and create a more comfortable environment and attitude toward menstruation. Being conscious of the potentially harmful impact of period instruments like pads on the environment, they aim to ensure that their methods are environmentally friendly. Periods have historically played the role of the barrier, not only in the form of the various side effects (cramps, fatigue) but also in the way of taboos and societal pressure, inhibiting women from doing ordinary tasks such as cooking. Gradually, women are learning to break barriers. Female athletes continue to train, young girls do not stop going to school, and we all teach ourselves not to be treated differently and isolated for an ordinary body function.

I loved the pulse and twinkle in their eyes as they spoke. They were so passionate about what they were doing, and when they talked about their daughter's project, I had a feeling I saw the future. I had met lots of founders of great programs for women, and I loved it, but this was one of the most inspiring. Not only because of what they were doing, but because it came from two young high school girls who did not wait for their turn to make a difference. They just did it.

I loved hearing them talk about how women were using their products, what they hoped to do next, and how much more they needed to grow.

Later, when I returned to Seattle, I was surprised to see a message from Vrisha Vyas, cofounder of STaMP. She wrote that she was excited to hear about my book because she is also very passionate about seeing women from every background lead. She wrote:

> While the different waves of feminism have paved a better life and path for today's woman, her challenges are by no means a thing of the past. From more professional issues such as wage gaps and unsafe work environments to more personal matters such as the still prevalent dowry system and other unrealistic societal expectations, women continue to fight for equal access to opportunities. Looking back, we would not have been able to develop this NGO and give back to society if we had not spoken up and shared our ideas. I would tell my young self that no idea is perfect at its inception, but you discuss and reflect. Maybe, it is ultimately successful. Perhaps, it may fail. Maybe, another idea stems from it. However, women who get an opportunity to grow should always strive to pave the road for the rest.

People like Vrisha and Hinal are what we need to keep the winds of change blowing. The tremendous growth in experiences and opportunities has occurred for women due to these grassroots movements happening everywhere in the world. The common goal of all of them is to create a culture conducive to every gender's ability to grow.

Second generation US immigrants are setting an excellent example for women following their passions without barriers and trying to bring the wave of change further. One example is Priyanka Jain Vora, a doctor of physical therapy specializing in women's/pelvic health rehab at Swedish Medical Center in Seattle. She was born and raised as a second-generation Indian in Boston, Massachusetts, where she was surrounded by a family of innovators and healthcare providers. She found her niche in women's health physical therapy when she began treating new mothers and realized how underserved they were. Expectations of mothers in modern society are to "bounce back" after giving birth, now known as the "fourth trimester." Specialists like Priyanka are devoted to delivering prenatal/postpartum care, treatment of back/pelvic pain, abdominal weakness, urinary/fecal incontinence, bowel dysfunction, pain with intercourse, pelvic organ prolapse, pelvic floor muscle dysfunction, and lactation pain to help patients return to full function. She states that research by the National Institutes of Health found that one out of every four women suffers from a pelvic floor muscle dysfunction in their lifetime. Many believe their symptoms are "normal" and don't seek help. In some European countries, physical therapy is prescribed as a mandatory part of postpartum care—so why not in the US?

"What shocks me every day," said Priyanka, "is how little women know about the changes our bodies undergo throughout the lifespan. I aspire to standardize postpartum physical therapy care across the nation and advance the accessibility of preventive and rehabilitative pelvic health care for all individuals."

But there is more to Priyanka than excelling in her field. Although she is a dedicated healthcare provider, amazingly, she has not compromised her passion along the way. That passion is dancing. In Seattle, she is well known as the founder of a Bollywood fusion dance company, Rangeela. She spent her childhood in eleven years of rigorous Bharatnatyam training, performed her Arangetram at age sixteen, captained her collegiate fusion dance team, taught Bollywood fitness classes, and choreographed and judged for national showcases. Nothing stopped her from following her passion.

Through her dance company, Priyanka provides a platform for South Asian dancers and choreographers to collaborate and share their passion for movement and music. The company specializes in performing and visual arts, teaching dance workshops, and creating original choreography for special events. Priyanka's uncompromising passion earned her recognition in the Smithsonian "Beyond Bollywood" exhibit at Seattle's Museum of History & Industry (MOHAI) titled, "How Indian Americans Shape The Nation."

Even first-generation women are not far behind when it comes to breaking the mold. Gunjan Kuthiala is a super-enthusiastic woman in the film and entertainment industry. When I met her, she was filming *Grey Stories* (an anthology story film) with some of the best-known actors of our time. I was trying to learn production during those days, and we were working on a sequel. I was amazed to learn she gave up a six-figure career in a Fortune 500 company. She always had creative aspirations as a writer, but in 2004, when she came to the US, she got lost in a nine to five job. "I always had a creative itch but got into HR, thinking I will never be able to make it as a writer or actor being an immigrant in the US. When I tried to explore the right platform for my talents, there was nothing available that could encourage or support me in my pursuits. It took a few more years of stabilizing my footing for financial stability. Only after that, I could pay attention to my inner voice, which was urging me to follow my true passion of writing, acting, and producing films inspired by real life." She went to Mumbai in 2018 to sign her production contract with Shemaroo (Bollywood filmmaking and distribution house). Simultaneously, she tried exploring acting opportunities with topmost casting directors and was disappointed to see the casting couch firsthand. "I faced situations that embarrassed me as female," she said. She became determined to return to the US and go full blast with her production company here; now, one year later, her production house is making headlines. "I am a mother of two in my late thirties and had a drastic change in my career to follow my dream. Being a woman, how you think matters. You can break the mold anytime. But it has to come from you. All you need is to believe in your dreams. My experience with barriers as a creative woman fueled my mission to create NRILIFE Productions. This much-needed platform can give opportunities to people based on their talent and creative aspirations, irrespective of their backgrounds or experience." Gunjan is committed to expanding her productions and setting an example for middle-aged, first-generation mothers. "Take baby steps and ask the Universe for what you want. Don't be shy. You got this." Women like Gunjan are breaking molds every day and providing encouraging examples as waves of feminism emerge higher.

When it comes to women as a whole group, the path to equality may be in sight, but a lot of work must still be done. We have no other place but to rise from where we currently are. Losing momentum is not even an option since we have just begun. I do see more bright spots now than ever before. Although a growing body of research exists on how to support diversity and inclusion effectively, the experiences and solutions for women of color and immigrants cannot be generalized under the umbrella of every woman in the workplace. It needs a specific angle and perspective. It is impossible to know what the best practices are without knowing the primary trouble spot is in the talent pipeline.

Do Not Let Your Voice Become an Echo

I began the journey of this book by talking about "finding your why." My goal throughout the book is to examine the leadership gap issues for women of color and find ways to tackle them. The best tool to bridge the gap is to have a voice, a loud voice. And to be able to use your voice, you must know "why" it matters to speak up. If we do not challenge what stops us, we all will be stuck in vicious circles of injustice. That is the difference between voice and echo. Sometimes when we choose not to speak up, we want to look agreeable so that we receive validation—and if that becomes our hidden psychology, then there is the only endless echo of unfairness in our silence or words. Women must never combine their fight for equity with the motive of saying things to look good. Everyone who identifies themselves as leaders must champion the strength of voice. They must have a tone of altruism. True leaders do not speak *their* cause. They speak the cause. They also amplify the voices for the cause.

The power of a strong voice is not meant as a special gift for a few people. We all must cultivate it to pay our price to witness the disparities. We often say people who discriminate are the problem, but the urge to consider ourselves superior to others is the actual problem. We all must strive to overcome this urge. When we can't become partners to end discrimination, we inadvertently make those gaps bigger. It is time for women who have made it into the workforce to start troubleshooting the path to leadership from the inside out. Paying it forward isn't only for women in the C-suite. It is for every woman who has learned something new about breaking into the system that kept her away for so long. It is for every woman who has dreamed big and knows her challenges well. It is for every woman who sees every woman like her giving up on her dreams without a fight. It is time for every woman to contribute forward by creating a new culture where an inclusive future can grow from infancy.

EVERYONE WHO IDENTIFIES THEMSELVES AS LEADERS MUST CHAMPION THE STRENGTH OF VOICE.

The momentum of change for women like me is in the very early stages. To make it a full-grown reality, it will take raising a village. There is a proven advantage when women can connect with other women of a similar background. We can only understand and empathize with those who have gone through similar experiences. These experiences help to create a culture of their own, including methods that can be applied to everyone and work as efficiently for them. Variation in results is the most unreliable factor, which is why we need the concept of equity. While equality has its perks, equity can be pretty advantageous in certain areas.

EVERY FRIEND I MADE TAUGHT ME A LOT ABOUT SURVIVING HERE IN THE US AS A FIRST-GENERATION IMMIGRANT.

As a woman wanting to make a difference in this world, every friend I made taught me a lot about surviving here in the US as a first-generation immigrant. I built up the courage to start my family and raise my kids without alienating them from their culture in this country. I needed to keep them deeply rooted in their culture while they lived a better life filled with opportunities. Every parent holds one wish and only one desire in their hearts for their children—they hope their child lives a better life than they did, and I want my children raised in an environment that does not rob them of opportunities. I felt comfortable going to work with my kids in daycare because I knew who I was doing it for. It took a long time for me to adjust, but it also helped me realize it was not entirely impossible. Every one of us can mold ourselves according to our situations if we try hard enough. I had to accept that my children will lead lives in an environment different from mine, but I have faith in my upbringing as well. The only reason I don't feel as insecure as other first-generation US immigrants may feel is I believe in myself and my ability to provide for my children.

But I did not reach this point alone. I had support from my friends and everyone around me who made my life easier as I settled in this country. Every woman who was in the same boat as I was helped me become a better version of myself. They gave me helpful advice, and my journey became smoother with some friends at my side. I have listed numerous examples in this book of moral support, some from personal experience. They reflect the power of the community—the power of the people you choose to be with. I was lucky enough to come across other women like me, but it makes me wonder if every other woman out there in the US is getting the same amount of attention and care I did. Of course, some parts of my life, some realities, I had to face alone, but having a shoulder to lean on was still helpful.

I know that holding a position of leadership does not solely qualify women to be mentors. It is the experience gained—the craft honed—that helps them become the mentors we need. This experience prepares women for imparting their acquired knowledge to help pull others across the not-so-imaginary gender line. These women can be essential assets to help others who are still unable to beat bias and prejudice in their lives.

Raising a Village: Equity Needs a Tribe

We all have experienced barriers in some form at some point in our lives. We all get to know it enough to be averse to it. The biggest fear we associate with barriers is that we will lose opportunities to grow or connect. But not all of us know what it means to be left entirely out.

That is why I embrace my role as a case manager for my patients. Two years ago, I changed my job profile from a director of rehab to a home health provider. When I worked in a nursing home, I was always excited about the day patients were discharged to their homes after a successful rehabilitation. But I was curious about how they did at home. Most of my senior patients told me they lived alone. I wanted to explore how they integrated themselves into the community and managed their chronic conditions. I started providing home health services in my community to elderly people with severe disabilities and chronic health issues. I could then see how they function in their home with or without support. Even during a pandemic, I continued to serve my patients in their homes, being an essential healthcare provider. But the most significant challenge I have seen them face is not physical; it is their need to offer what they can and be appreciated. We all can suffer deprivation, but if we lose the feeling of worthiness, that is the most detrimental to our survival.

Belonging is a feeling that flourishes based on what we can contribute. This consciousness is indispensable to inclusion. Therefore, everyone must have a sense of ability to grow and develop their potential to thrive. That's the real magic of inclusion—everyone blossoms and delivers their best. So, if anyone needs help to blossom, then we must collectively help them.

That is why I say we need to raise a village to support equity

I am putting together a list of simple steps women can take to create a village of their own, no matter where they are, to work toward fixing the broken systems that don't work for them. This list can help them step up so they can pay it forward to help every woman reach their potential.

1. Igniting Conversations

Igniting conversations is the best way to expand horizons for women and help them promote diversity and inclusion. The real problem begins when we tell women not to raise their voices when it comes to a specific topic. Often, women are barred from a particular conversation because people believe it is beyond their capability of understanding. I have seen this take place many times to me and others. Many women are either afraid to raise their voices or fear the humiliation that comes with their voice falling on deaf ears.

Talking about problems is the first step toward finding a solution. How can we tackle such issues if we do not even address them?

We need to create a culture that expands the horizon for women, promotes diversity and inclusion, and keeps women safe from gender-based violence. This process will require a new wave of culture that has learned its lesson. We often see history repeating itself in certain areas, so we must learn from past mistakes. We need to keep an open mind and take action now so it is easier for women to feel secure in everything they do.

This change will not take place overnight. It requires immense effort. It will require working from the bottom and steadily making our way to the top. Whenever a woman is labeled bossy or abrasive, mansplained to, or man-interrupted, ask yourself what needs to be done. Labels only cause more doubts for women and make them wonder if they should even bother to counterattack. When they do, they are then labeled as aggressive and are often told to calm down. Speaking up in those critical moments is essential. It needs to be adequately addressed.

The real problem lies in the lack of confidence women have whenever they are interrupted.

2. Keeping Conversations Transparent

What's hard for women is conversations that sugarcoat the problems. "Oh, it's not that bad, though." People may downplay the talk because they do not want to come across as problematic. We need to keep conversations transparent and address the problem at hand rather than tiptoeing around it. Tiptoeing creates more problems in the end. Without transparency, women will forever remain conscious of what they do and say because society has trained them to be more reserved and conservative.

This self-doubt is hammered into women from a very young age. I want to see that change; I don't want girls to be always pressured to attain higher grades, yet be quiet when meaningful conversations occur at dinner tables or in classrooms.

Keeping conversations transparent can help us reach a solution faster than one might imagine. There is no need for you to hide behind diplomatic armor and sugarcoat things because you are afraid of being labeled as something. We need to change the concept of labeling women when they are speaking their minds. No, we are not too problematic, unreasonable, and aggressive when we point out that women's voices often go unheard in public and professional places. Whenever someone tries to cut you off in the middle of the conversation, you can show them you are not yet done speaking and openly address this issue.

3. Finding Ways to Make Workplaces Work for Women

One of the biggest problems women face is the unbearable working environment. The competition is not what makes it unacceptable for women, but rather the dirty politics between colleagues and employees. Women often find their workplaces unbearable due to the patriarchy evident in the workplace.

What we can do to raise our village is to try to make the workplace workable for women. We can show women that they can come forward if they are facing specific issues in their workplaces. Every human, regardless of gender and race, deserves to be treated with respect in their workplace.

4. Coming Together Every Chance You Get

People look for many reasons to go in different directions, but it only takes us to come together every chance we get. Women must confide in other women to help them ease their burdens. You can be that woman for them by exuding an inviting and warm aura. We all seek comfort from platonic relationships at some point. Be the woman who can lend her shoulder to another woman to rest her head for a while.

Make sure you always call out to the women who seek mentoring from you and invite them over whenever you get the chance.

Life can be hectic and busy, but we all deserve a break. Make sure you come together and stay in touch with each other every chance you get. Being there can make all the difference for someone who is suffering silently. Hold a meeting just to check on them and ask how their progress is going. This way is the best to reassure women and guide them on how to deal with certain situations that arise in both personal and professional environments.

5. Reassessing and Updating Goals

By meeting and talking frequently, you and the women under you can come together to reevaluate and update goals with each other. It is essential to talk about their goals daily to help remind them why they started on this journey to lead. Dealing with a strenuous amount of work can drain anyone and demotivate them. It can make them forget why they started this journey. It is vital to help the women under your leadership to discuss and reassess their goals.

It is a difficult task to get to the end goal of women having their fair share in leading positions. As we fight to transform a culture based on inequality, our challenge grows tougher. We have to push the envelope every day by discovering new allies and working on opportunities to create new partners. We can't exclude anyone, even those who are barriers on the path to inclusion.

TAKEAWAYS

I have belonged to various groups of women throughout my life—as a young woman in a developing country, as an immigrant woman, as a first-generation woman, as a married woman, as a mother raising multicultural kids, as an educated but jobless woman, as a woman getting promoted to a senior position, as a woman of color, as a woman who wants to fight for equity. I realize the diversity of my experiences as I write this book. And I thank the men and women who inspired me and gave me hope in every stage and every group which I have identified for myself. But I will say that I still seek conversations with and insight from my female friends, especially the ones who have walked beside me on the paths we shared. I do not mean that I exclude men when I seek support and progress. Absolutely not. This book is not about giving everything to women and taking everything from men. It is about awareness for achieving balance and fairness. And for that cohort of women, it is essential to trigger the change we need. If women continue to take a secondary role, progress will elude all of us.

Inclusion will require work, especially for women from the minority, and it needs sustenance. It needs results, which not only stay but also multiply, and that cannot happen if women position themselves above or below everyone—they need to work with everyone. We have more women in the workforce than ever before, and all of them can be great influencers when it comes to leadership. They have the power to determine their path, and they don't need to work alone. When we face a challenge as massive as inequality, systemic and structural racism, and sexism, we have to work in full force. We have to find strength and create it as well. We need to unite to complete the circle as we move along the path to inclusion, equity, and breaking the concrete ceiling.

SELF-REFLECTION EXERCISE:
PAYING IT FORWARD

1. What is your ideal vision for gender equality in the world?

    _____

    _____

    _____

2. Have you witnessed disparity in opportunities around you for yourself or others? What support have you found or extended to others to gain access to opportunities?

    _____

    _____

    _____

    _____

3. What are the main reasons for the modern leadership gap in your experience?

    _____

    _____

    _____

4. Do you have good time-management practices to make room to support people in need?

    _____

    _____

    _____

5. What is the best way you think you can give back to your community?

    _____

    _____

    _____

AFTERWORD

I sincerely hope I have been able to put together a compelling narrative of why it is crucial to understand diverse women's workplace experiences. Women as a group are not monolithic. The causes of under-representation at top positions also vary. I have used curated reports to show the facts and figures to highlight the disparity in opportunities. But more data and research is needed on how gender and race affect advancement and growth. Women constitute a majority of the US population, yet they lag substantially behind men when it comes to leadership positions. Gender equality is still a goal, even in this mighty nation. The world's highest ceiling is still not shattered, and we have yet to welcome a female president. This ceiling becomes even more significant for women of color because they are woefully underrepresented in C-suites and decision-making posts.

An empowered woman will uplift the world. But that is only the beginning. Our main goal as humans is not to fight for justice but to develop empathy. A fight without empathy is nothing more than a remedy. And when it comes to equality, there is no easy fix. A society where any segment gets marginalized must evoke a sense of unrest for all. We can't win if half of us are always losing. Therefore,

I emphasize understanding the gap in opportunities, especially for minority women.

The sense of overcoming inequality will make us one strong world.

This sense will keep anyone from creating borders around resources and prospects. That is the goal of this book. Equality is the path, not the destination. I am not saying we have to give up what we have to achieve equity. I am urging us all to work for systems that connect our growths. Because when we connect, we rise.

Discrimination leads to exploitation and division. Division can create a false sense of superiority, which is the root cause of apathy. This indifference is the biggest human evil. To erase this evil, people at all levels must join hands.

That is the theme of this book.

Last year, when I started working on this book, I got a call from a woman I knew through a mutual friend. She told me she wanted to know more about my book. I invited her to my home to talk over a cup of coffee. I was stunned by what she told me.

She shared that she had immigrated to the US after marriage but, within a year, became homeless. It was due to domestic violence and abuse. She had to sleep on the streets with an infant because she had no one to protect her and no place to go. She was so scared of her spouse that she did not even ask for child support. She just wanted safety and a way to survive even if that meant on the streets. I became overly emotional hearing about her struggle. In Chapter 2, I told you the story of Kanchan, who dared to ask for what she wanted. But what about a woman who needs to find the courage to fight injustice?

This woman told me that nothing in her life could have prepared her for the challenge she faced as an unsheltered mother. She had to pick apart her life piece by piece to put it together for herself and her daughter. She is currently a proud single mother and works as an executive in a local firm. Her courage came from her infant daughter, whom she had to protect from violence right from the time of her birth.

Her example made me melt inside that day. Her bravery and persistence warmed my heart. I felt so bonded with her. And in my private moments, more clarity emerged. I may be one person who feels empowered by writing a book about gender bias and inequality, but I need courage to deal with the challenges and bring that change to people around me. She showed me we all have courage, but we can find it only when we focus on solutions more than the problem. This insight is the power of connection. Different circumstances and struggles can still unite two people and spark inspiration to emerge from the odds.

We all need a legacy of fairness to give away to our generations. We all have bonds to make to lift the world.

RISING TOGETHER
AS A TRIBE

"Yesterday I was clever, so I wanted to change the world.
Today I am wise, so I am changing myself."

— Rumi

A beautiful dream has come true for me by writing this book—my dream to spread the message about coming together to achieve equality. You can experience this dream's beauty, just like me, by recommending this book to your friends, family, and anyone in your workspace. Change may appear collective, but it is subtle. It happens one day, one heart, and one action at a time. Most importantly, it begins with you. Therefore, I encourage you to build the tribe around this cause of gender equity by forming a *Why She Must Lead* book club or discussion circle. Please visit www.WhySheMustLead.com to order bulk copies. I have also compiled additional free resources like helpful hints for Self-Reflection Exercises in this book. Additionally, there are DEI PowerPoints for presentations to provide tools to advocate for racial and gender equity. I also invite you to join my private community by emailing me. In solidarity!

— Vasudha Sharma

LEAD THE CHANGE IN YOUR ORGANIZATION:
DIVERSITY, EQUITY, AND INCLUSION

KEYNOTE, WORKSHOP, EVENT, OR TRAINING

Your team members, employees, staff, managers, executives, recruiters, and trainees can take away a wealth of information and resources to experience the power of inclusivity and connections. Vasudha's *Lead the Change* message in a live group workshop, training, event, or keynote will inspire a positive impact through targeted and high-involvement diversity practices in terms of current business and cultural challenges.

TAKEAWAYS

- Develop awareness of existing DEI practices in your organization and their effectiveness

- Formulate an objective measure for employee-engagement levels

- Apply your findings to enhance organizational culture in your team and company

- Recognize barriers like unconscious bias and how it affects the way people perceive and react to others

- Review stereotypes and prejudices that may influence behavior in groups

- Learn tools and methods to improve the psychological wellness of all employees

- Understand the advantages of diversity and why it matters in your organization

- Examine strategies for implementing and adhering to ethical standards

This workshop is for anyone interested in creating an inclusive and compassionate culture that promotes fairness, equal opportunities, and treatment of employees and associates.

To learn more, email connect@vasudhasharma.com.

EVERYONE HAS A STORY TO SHARE

The Art and Gift of Storytelling (TAGS) Program by Vasudha Sharma

Storytelling is an ancient and valuable art that extends around the globe to connect and create an impact. When you share your story, you create an influence that can touch many lives in the present and future.

Vasudha has created a Storytelling Program to concentrate on vision, message, and performance skills. You can learn this craft to pursue a professional storytelling career, to enhance your presentations or talks, to foster conversation across diverse populations, or to enhance professional work performance as managers, educators, community workers, human resource leaders, formal trainers, healers, counselors, and social justice workers. The program has a guided approach to appreciate the art of storytelling, objectively analyze key features of a well-told story, prepare you to perform your storytelling art on various platforms, and refine your ability and gift of gab.

The objectives of the complete step-by-step program are:

- Forming clarity and untangling messages to develop a story
- Preparing a story for the audience

- Outlining gestures, expressions, and relatable content
- Applying the details to build interest
- Enhancing presentation skills to generate your following
- Applying marketing and media coaching to build your community

To learn more about this program, visit:
www.vasudhasharma.com/tags

ORGANIZATIONS READERS CAN SUPPORT

I have listed below some of the organizations I have had the opportunity to get connected with. They are working for crucial issues of diversity, education, health, and feminine hygiene. If you want to know more about them, kindly visit their websites and learn the ways you can get involved.

Voice Of Planet

www.thevoiceofplanet.com

Making Communities inclusive is a vital part of the Voice of Planet. Their mission is to celebrate diversity and advocate for inclusion and equity by promoting cultural activities and community outreach.

Sukarya

www.GiveSukaryaUS.org

Established in 1998, Sukarya is a women-centric and women-led GuideStar Platinum-certified grassroots level NGO. This organization is working in the area of Maternal Child Health & Nutrition as well as Education & Empowerment of women, children, and adolescent girls living in the slums and hard-to-reach villages of India in Delhi, Haryana, and Rajasthan. It has served more than six million women and children living in six hundred-plus villages and one hundred-plus slums. It looks up to individuals, foundations, and corporations for support. Email: sukarya@sukarya.org.

STaMP

www.stampngo.org

This non-profit is a unique initiative to address the lack of resources for females during their menstrual cycle in India. They work on methods to make sanitary pads readily available and affordable. Their goal is to reach the poor and backward class of society. Their efforts are environment-friendly as well.

ACKNOWLEDGMENTS

The process of writing this book has brought so much insight and depth into my quest to explore leadership when it comes to women like me, who are mothers, full-time employees, women of color, and first-generation immigrants.

My sincere thanks,

- To my husband, Puneet, who inspired me to write this book. You define what love and commitment can do to make dreams come true. Thank you for the daily morning cardamom tea just the way I like it, your smile and enthusiasm during my crazy late-night discussions, your positive comments, and your honest feedback on my drafts, as I wrote.

- To my parents, thank you for instilling spirituality in me and helping me to hold on to my moral compass closely. I am forever grateful for your unconditional love and support in my life wherever I may be.

- To visionary coach Christine Gail, thank you for instilling confidence and discipline in me. You are the best accountability partner anyone could get.

- To my brilliant editors Tyler Tichelaar and Larry Alexander, your guidance has been indispensable for this book.

- To creative book cover designer Kerry Jesberger for aligning with my vision and this book.

- To layout designers Shiloh Schroeder, Rachel Langaker, and Sherdellah Anunciado.

- To my friend San D Nath for my author's portrait and always amazing me with your talents.

- To my brother Alok Sharma and my sister-in-law Veenu Sharma for always providing me with motivational support during long distance phone calls and video chats from Delhi.

- To all the women who gave their time to give interviews so I could grasp an understanding of leadership and its many aspects, I thank you from the bottom of my heart.

I am grateful to Dr. Aditi Govitrikar, who took her precious time to learn about my book and endorsed it with her Foreword. I am honored and humbled to have received so much support from iconic women leaders like Manka Dhingra and Mona Das during this book's journey. Thank you for the coffee conversations and meetups.

I have been fortunate to meet numerous men and women who have taught me integral lessons that shaped my life. Thank you, Sunita Pillai, for taking the time to devise surveys for this book. My thanks go to my teachers at Montfort School, New Delhi, India, and my close childhood friends, Deepti Kautish and Aarti Gupta. Thank you to my very special college girlfriends Meenakshi Pandey, Anjali Sarna, and Ankur Kler, for showing me the power of laughter and care to build unbreakable bonds.

I would like to thank my mentors and role models who inspired me to use my voice for social causes. My abundant gratitude to

Charmaine Slye and Stephanie Wright for giving me precious guidance and coaching to deliver my message on various platforms. Special thanks to Debdutta Dash, Meera Satpathy, Gunjan Kuthiala, and Benita Horn. My gratitude for your guidance is boundless.

REFERENCES

Alter, A. (2019). 2 Reasons Women of Color Are Leaving Your Company. NEW. Retrieved from: https://www.newonline.org/news-insights/blog/diversity/2-reasons-women-color-are-leaving-your-company

Britannica. (2020). Lakshmi Bai. Website. Retrieved from: https://www.britannica.com/biography/Lakshmi-Bai

Brookings. (2020). The US Will Become Minority White in 2045, Census Projects. Website. Retrieved from: https://www.brookings.edu/blog/the-avenue/2018/03/14/the-us-will-become-minority-white-in-2045-census-projects/

Burke, Tarana. #MeToo Was Started for Black and Brown Women and Girls. They're Still Being Ignored. *Washington Post* (Nov. 9, 2017): https://www.washingtonpost.com/news/post-nation / wp/2017/11/09/the-waitress-who-works-in-the-diner-needs-to-know-that-the-issue-of -sexual-harassment-is-about-her-too [https://perma.cc/22XR-GUEJ].

Cavanaugh. C. (2018). A Brief History: The Four Waves of Feminism. Progressive Women Leadership. Retrieved from: https://www.progressivewomensleadership.com/a-brief-history-the-four-waves-of-feminism/

Center for Reproductive Rights (2020). Legislation on Female Genital Mutilation in the United States. Retrieved from: https://www.reproductiverights.org/sites/default/files/documents/pub_bp_fgmlawsusa.pdf

Charts that show the glaring gap between men and women's salaries in the US Sonam Sheth, Shayanne Gal and Andy Kiersz Aug 26, 2019, 6:16 PM, https://www.businessinsider.com/gender-wage-pay-gap-charts-2017-3#women-with-children-gain-no-salary-boost-while-men-with-children-are-rewarded-5

Chira, S (2018). Numbers Hint at Why #MeToo Took Off: The Sheer Number Who Can Say Me Too. *The New York Times.* Retrieved from: https://www.nytimes.com/2018/02/21/upshot/pervasive-sexual-harassment-why-me-too-took-off-poll.html

Cockburn, C., & Ormrod, S. (1993). Gender and Technology in the Making. SAGE Publications Ltd.

Employment Rate of Women in the U.S 1990-2000 https://www.statista.com/statistics/192396/employment-rate-of-women-in-the-us-since-1990/

Femtech Leaders. (2019). The Top 10 Famous Female Leaders in History. Website Retrieved from http://www.femtechleaders.com/the-top-10-famous-female-leaders-in-history/

Forbes. (2019). The World's 100 Most Powerful Women. Website. Retrieved from: https://www.forbes.com/power-women/#25c8f27d5e25

Future for Us. (2020). Welcome to the Future of Work. Website. Retrieved from: https://futureforus.co/

Gates, M. (2020). Gender equality is within our reach. Evoke. Retrieved from: https://www.evoke.org/articles/september-2019/gender-equality-is-within-our-reach

Harris, Carla. (2014) *Strategize to Win: The New Way to Start Out, Step Up, or Start Over in Your Career*. New York, NY: Hudson Street Press.

Harris, Carla. (2016) *Expect to Win: 10 Proven Strategies for Thriving in the Workplace*. New York, NY: Plume.

Hodges, B. D. (2018). Learning from Dorothy Vaughan: artificial intelligence and the health professions. *Med Educ*, 52(1), 11-3.

Huff Post. (2020). Amy Bhatt. Website. Retrieved from: https://www.huffpost.com/author/amy-bhatt

Ibarra, H., Carter, N. M., & Silva, C. (2010). Why men still get more promotions than women. *Harvard Business Review*, 88(9), 80-85.

Jacobs, T. (2019). Men Are Judged Based on Their Potential; Women Are Judged Based on Their Past Performance. *Pacific Standard*. Retrieved from: https://psmag.com/economics/men-are-judged-based-on-their-potential-women-are-judged-based-on-their-past-performance

Jeffcoat, S (2008). Mentoring Women of Color for Leadership: Do Barriers Exist? Retrieved from: https://etd.ohiolink.edu/!etd.send_file?accession=antioch1220894689&disposition=inline

John, J. (2020). How Jacinda Ardern Became New Zealand's Youngest Female Prime Minister. National Builder. Retrieved from: https://nationbuilder.com/jacinda_ardern

Kickstarter. (2020). *Knock Down the House: A Documentary*. Website. Retrieved from: https://www.kickstarter.com/projects/949597697/knock-down-the-house-a-documentary

Livingston, B. and Opie, T. (2019). Even at "Inclusive" Companies, Women of Color Don't Feel Supported. *Harvard Business Review*. Retrieved from: https://hbr.org/2019/08/even-at-inclusive-companies-women-of-color-dont-feel-supported

Mohr, T. (2014). Why Women Don't Apply for Jobs Unless They're 100 percent Qualified. *Harvard Business Review*. Retrieved from: https://hbr.org/2014/08/ why-women-dont-apply-for-jobs-unless-theyre-100-qualified

National Portal of India. (2020). Constitution of India. Website. Retrieved from: https://www.india.gov.in/my-government/ constitution-india

Ogden, L. (2019). Working Mothers Face, A 'Wall' Of Bias—But There Are Ways To Push Back. *Science Mag*. Retrieved from: https://www.sciencemag.org/careers/2019/04/ working-mothers-face-wall-bias-there-are-ways-push-back

Ossola, Alexendra. (2019). The thing women struggle with most at work isn't sexism, it's ageism. Quartz. Retrieved from: https://qz.com/1742646/ ageism-not-sexism-is-becoming-womens-biggest-work-concern/

PayScale. (2020). The State of the Gender Pay Gap. 2019. Website. Retrieved from: https://www.payscale.com/data/ gender-pay-gap#section02

Pifer, R. (2019). Women make up only 13 percent of healthcare CEOs. Healthcare Drive. Retrieved from: https://www.healthcaredive.com/news/ women-make-up-only-13-of-healthcare-ceos/545469/

Prison Policy Initiative (2020): https://www.prisonpolicy.org/reports/outofwork.html#methodology percent20for percent20sources percent20and percent20data percent20notes.

Psychology Today. (2020). Perfectionism. Website. Retrieved from: https://www.psychologytoday.com/intl/basics/perfectionism

R. Max & R. H. (2019). Urbanization. Our World in Data. Retrieved from: https://ourworldindata.org/urbanization#share-of-people-living-in-slums

Senate Democrats. (2020). About Mona. Website. Retrieved from: http://sdc.wastateleg.org/das/biography/

Shetterley, M. L. *Hidden Figures*. New York: Harper Collins 2016.

Siddick, S. (2019). A Future for Us by US. YWCA. Retrieved from: https://www.ywcaworks.org/blogs/ywca/wed-03062019-1108/future-us-us

State of Womxn of Color Summit. (2019). Splash That. Website. Retrieved from: https://thestateofwomxnofcolorsummit.splashthat.com/

The Riveter. (2019). New Mothers Need More Support When They Return to Work. Period. Website. Retrieved from: https://theriveter.co/voice/new-mothers-need-more-support-when-they-return-to-work-period/

The World Bank. (2020). School Enrollment Primary Female. Website. Retrieved from: https://data.worldbank.org/indicator/SE.PRM.ENRR.FE

Ultrasound Schools Info. (2020). Does the Gender Pay Gap Exist in Healthcare? Website. Retrieved from: https://www.ultrasound-schoolsinfo.com/does-the-gender-pay-gap-exist-in-healthcare/

Washington, Z. (2019). Women of Color Get Less Support at Work. Here's How Managers Can Change That. *Harvard Business Review*. Retrieved from: https://hbr.org/2019/03/women-of-color-get-less-support-at-work-heres-how-managers-can-change-that

WFF. (2020). Accelerate the Advancement of Women Leaders in the Food Industry. Website. Retrieved from: https://wff.org/Home/NewsMore

ABOUT THE AUTHOR

Vasudha Sharma is an author, keynote speaker, storyteller, coach, Diversity, Equity, and Inclusion (DEI) advocate, wellness expert, and Doctor of Physical Therapy.

She enjoys working on DEI strategies as a member of the mayor's inclusion task force in Renton, Washington. She has been an avid blog writer and contributor to many columns published in newspapers serving the Asian and Indian population. She is also the founder of the non-profit Voice of Planet, with a mission to promote inclusion through cultural activities and community outreach.

Vasudha is originally from New Delhi, India, and currently resides in the suburbs of Seattle with her husband Puneet and their two boys Krish and Vansh.

For more information about Vasudha Sharma, visit:
VasudhaSharma.com
WhySheMustLead.com

SPEAKING, WORKSHOPS, AND MEDIA INQUIRIES:
connect@vasudhasharma.com

FOLLOW VASUDHA ON SOCIAL MEDIA:
facebook.com/whyshemustlead
Instagram: @vasudhausa
Twitter: @vasudhasvoice
#WhySheMustLead
#VasudhaSpeaks

A free ebook edition is available with the purchase of this book.

To claim your free ebook edition:

1. Visit MorganJamesBOGO.com
2. Sign your name CLEARLY in the space
3. Complete the form and submit a photo of the entire copyright page
4. You or your friend can download the ebook to your preferred device

Morgan James BOGO™

A **FREE** ebook edition is available for you or a friend with the purchase of this print book.

CLEARLY SIGN YOUR NAME ABOVE

Instructions to claim your free ebook edition:
1. Visit MorganJamesBOGO.com
2. Sign your name CLEARLY in the space above
3. Complete the form and submit a photo of this entire page
4. You or your friend can download the ebook to your preferred device

Print & Digital Together Forever.

Snap a photo

Free ebook

Read anywhere